30 UNDER 30

30 Essential Lessons to Learn by Age 30

DUSTIN VALENTE

First printing, 2026.
Selfpublishing.com

ISBN: 979-8-90057-216-1 - Ebook
ISBN: 979-8-90057-217-8 - Paperback
ISBN: 979-8-90057-218-5 - Hardcover

"The happiness of your life depends upon the quality of your thoughts."

— Marcus Aurelius

CONTENTS

Part IV: Fitness

Part V: Finance

INTRODUCTION

I didn't write this book because I have everything figured out. I wrote it because I don't, and neither does anyone else. What I do have are lessons I've come back to again and again, lessons learned through failure, observation, repetition, and growth.

Most people in their teens and twenties wrestle with the same questions. What does it mean to grow up? To succeed? To be happy? How do you actually build a life that feels solid?

Sure, there's endless content online telling you the "five habits" or the "one secret," but it's scattered, shallow, and often disconnected from real life. You're left piecing things together on your own, or scrolling until you see a meme that resonates with what you're dealing with and 2 mins later you can't remember what it

I wanted to create something different.

One book that brings everything together, organized in a way that actually makes sense.

This book is organized into five sections, Life, Love, Family, Fitness, and Finance, because those are the areas that quietly shape everything else. There's no fluff here, no guru energy, no motivational clichés. Just real lessons, grounded in experience, meant to be applied.

This isn't a one-time read. It's something you come back to when life shifts, when relationships change, when goals evolve, or when you need a reminder of what actually matters.

I'm not a twenty-five-year-old who sold a company for millions. I'm still figuring things out, still growing, still learning every day. I've made more mistakes than I can count, and instead of pretending otherwise, I decided to share what I've learned along the way.

If these lessons help you, or someone you care about, avoid even a few unnecessary detours, then writing this was worth it.

— Dustin Valente

LIFE

LEARN THE POWER OF DELAYED GRATIFICATION

Success hinges on your ability to resist short-term pleasure in exchange for long-term reward. Delayed gratification isn't just a skill. It's a mindset shift. It's the difference between people who talk about success and people who actually build it.

The Hard Truth I Learned

I learned this lesson the expensive way.

There was a season when I got pulled into day-trading hype. Options. GameStop. Crypto. The rush was unreal. Watching an account spike 50%, 70%, even 100% overnight makes you feel unstoppable, like you've cracked some secret code to wealth.

But what goes up fast usually comes down harder.

My account imploded, chasing fast money. No real strategy. Just hype, dopamine, and fear of missing out. I went from feeling like a market genius to realizing I was gambling, not building anything. That's where most people get stuck. They confuse excitement with effectiveness. They think success is about speed.

It's not.

Real success, the kind that lasts, is built slowly. It's built on patience, discipline, and compounding effort. Quick wins feel incredible in the moment, but they don't create anything durable. They're like sugar highs. A short rush, followed by a crash that leaves you worse off than before.

The Gym Principle Applies to Everything

This lesson isn't just about money. It applies to everything.

Think about fitness. You don't go to the gym for three days and wake up shredded. You don't eat one clean meal and expect your abs to show up. You lift weights for weeks without seeing much change. You eat well, skip dessert, go to bed early, and still look in the mirror wondering if it's working.

Something is changing. You just can't see it yet.

That's the moment most people quit. But if you keep going, if you stay consistent when there's no visible payoff, one day it shows up. The strength. The shape. The energy. The results appear after the work, not before it.

Fitness is one of the most honest teachers of delayed gratification. And what it teaches transfers everywhere: relationships, business, mental health, finances, purpose. Progress happens quietly. Growth is hidden. The payoff comes later. The people who win are the ones who keep showing up during the silence.

The Shift That Changed Everything

When I stepped back from chasing fast money, I realized something uncomfortable. Boring works.

Instead of gambling on volatile trades or the next big thing, what actually builds wealth is consistency over time. Automatic investing. Low-cost index funds. Letting compounding do the heavy lifting. It's not exciting, and that's exactly why it works.

The same principle applies everywhere in life. Want a great body? Skip the fad diets and ninety-day transformations. Show up four to five days a week. Eat clean. Sleep well. Do that for years. Want financial freedom? Choose the longer, safer path instead of sprinting along the edge of a cliff chasing shortcuts.

Sometimes the longer road isn't slower. It's just less risky.

Delayed gratification is the foundation of almost every goal worth achieving. The people who build meaningful lives aren't chasing constant stimulation or instant wins. They're willing to do the boring work longer than everyone else. And eventually, that patience compounds into something most people never reach.

Questions for Reflection

- Where am I still chasing short-term rewards instead of long-term growth?

- What's one area where I could apply more consistency this month?

- When have I seen slow, steady effort pay off—and how did it feel?

- If I stay on my current path, where will I be in five years? Would I be proud of that?

WRITE DOWN YOUR GOALS

Transforming goals from fleeting thoughts into tangible outcomes starts with one simple action: writing them down. It's not magic, it's strategy.

From Eye Rolls to "Ah-Ha"

When I first heard about writing down goals, I rolled my eyes. It sounded like fluffy advice you'd find on a motivational poster. My mom told me about it, and I remember thinking, *What do you mean I just write it down and it happens? That's ridiculous.*

And she wasn't wrong. Writing something down doesn't make it magically appear, the power isn't in the paper, it's in the intention.

When you take an idea floating around in your head and put it on paper, you change its status. It stops being a passing thought and becomes a commitment, you're telling your brain this matters, this is something I'm serious about. That shift alone forces you out of passive mode and into action.

Making Goals Real

I've written down income targets for specific years, net worth goals like hitting seven figures by a certain age, and even what I want in a partner, down to values, personality, and lifestyle. The point isn't manifesting in some mystical sense, the point is clarity.

Your mind is full of noise, ideas, distractions, comparisons, and pressure coming from every direction. If you don't capture what matters, it disappears. Writing things down cuts through that chaos and gives your goals a place to live outside your head, somewhere you can revisit them, refine them, and measure them.

Once a goal is written down, your subconscious starts working on it whether you realize it or not. You begin noticing opportunities, making decisions that align with it, and saying no to things that don't serve it. That's not luck, that's focus.

Clarity Creates Direction

Want to meet the right person? Be specific. What values do they have, how do they treat people, what kind of life do you want to build together? Write it down.

Want to make $200K in two years? Don't just think about the number, write it down. Break it apart, where does it come from, salary, commission, side income, investments. Seeing it in front of you turns a vague desire into a real target.

If you're struggling to come up with big goals, start small. Write down what you want to accomplish today or this week. The scale doesn't matter, the act of writing is the power, it trains your brain to operate with intention instead of reacting to whatever shows up.

The Annual Review That Changed Everything

Every December, I sit down and write out my goals for the next year, reviewing what worked, what didn't, and what I want more or less of. Some goals stay the same, like fitness or finances, while others evolve as life changes.

The surprising part is what happens when I look back a year later. I'm always shocked by how many goals I hit without consciously chasing them every day. That's alignment. When your goals are visible, your actions naturally start moving in that direction.

Not every goal hits on schedule, and that's something I had to learn the hard way. Paying off my student loans is a perfect example. When I graduated in 2016 with about $36,000 in debt, I wrote down a simple goal: get this paid off as fast as possible. At the time, I thought two years was realistic. It wasn't. My income was lower than I expected, the cost of living added up quickly, and life had other plans, but the goal stayed written down. Everytime I opened up my reminders on my phone I saw it constantly. Every time I reviewed my finances, it was there reminding me what I was working toward. Even when progress felt slow, the intention never disappeared.

It took longer than I originally planned, but it still happened, and that's the part that matters. Writing that goal down kept it alive when it would have been easy to push it off or justify doing something else with the money. It shaped the choices I made, the lifestyle I was willing to live with, and the discipline I had to build along the way. I go deeper later in the book on exactly how I paid it off and the tradeoffs I made to do it, but it all started with writing the goal down and refusing to let it fade into the background.

The timeline changed, the intention didn't.

Writing it down didn't make the debt disappear, it kept the goal alive long enough for reality to catch up. That's the real value. Writing your goals down doesn't guarantee speed, it guarantees direction.

Questions for Reflection

- Have I written down my goals in the last twelve months?

- Which current goals feel most aligned with who I want to become?

- How might my daily habits change if I reviewed my goals weekly?

- What are the things I always tell myself I want to do? What would happen if I wrote them down?

LISTEN MORE THAN YOU SPEAK

This might be the single life skill in this book that takes you further than almost anything else. The ability to shut up and actually listen, without interrupting, without planning your next response, without trying to sound smart, is one of the most underrated superpowers you can develop.

Some of the biggest improvements in my life started happening in my early to mid-twenties, especially in my career, when I stopped assuming I knew more than everyone else and started paying attention to what people were actually saying. I stopped trying to prove myself and started absorbing others, what I like to call "ear hustling."

Ear Hustling

Ear hustling is the ability to listen closely, extract the lesson, and apply it yourself.

When I first started in sales, I worked at a fintech company in business development. My first boss, Nathan Coleman, was a monster at virtual sales pitching and an elite conversationalist. He was always three steps ahead of the client, anticipating objections before they even finished forming them. While others were waiting for their turn to talk, he was listening for what *really* mattered.

I started paying attention to how he said things, when he said them, and what he didn't say at all. At first it felt awkward, like I was trying to mimic someone else instead of being myself. Over time, I put my own spin on it, keeping the underlying structure while making it natural to me. Once it became mine, my calls improved, my confidence went up, and my results followed.

It all started with listening first, trying something different, and being open to perspectives outside my own instead of swinging blindly and hoping for a home run.

Listen First, Act Later

This doesn't mean blindly doing whatever someone says because "Joe Schmoe" recommended it or your Aunt Betty swore by it. The lesson is to listen first and act later, knowing your odds improve when you pause instead of jumping in.

Mark Cuban is a great example of this on *Shark Tank*. If you watch closely, he's often the last person to speak. He listens to the entire pitch, absorbs what the other sharks are thinking and saying, then responds when he has the most information. That patience is a huge reason he's been so successful. He doesn't rush, he waits, then strikes with clarity.

Why This Changes Everything

True listening applies everywhere: sales, leadership, relationships, conflict resolution, consulting, medicine, law, and any situation where trust and influence matter.

Yet most people never master it. Regardless of age or intelligence, real listening is rare, which is exactly why it makes you stand out immediately.

The Interruption Trap

Let's be honest, we've all been guilty of this. Someone starts talking and halfway through you're itching to jump in. Maybe to relate, maybe to one-up them, maybe because silence makes you uncomfortable.

Growing up in an Italian household with two brothers, interruptions were normal. Sometimes it was excitement, sometimes competition, sometimes just fighting for the last word at the dinner table. The problem is that outside your family, it's annoying, and almost no one appreciates it.

When you slow down and let people talk, you get more out of the conversation. You ask better questions. You hear what they *actually* mean. People will often give you more information than you asked for if you simply give them space. This has been especially powerful in my sales career.

The Three-Second Rule That Changed Everything

Eventually I adopted a simple rule: wait three seconds after someone finishes speaking before responding.

That small habit turned choppy, ten-minute back-and-forth conversations into long, free-flowing discussions more times than I can count. When I feel the urge to jump in, I pause, let them finish, count to three, then respond. Often I ask a follow-up question instead of making a point.

At first it felt awkward, like I was being passive. That wasn't passivity, it was insecurity.

Silence isn't weakness, it's presence. And presence is rare, not just in high school or college, but well into professional life.

Elon Musk does this exceptionally well. Watch any interview and you'll notice how often he pauses before answering, processing every word before responding with intention. He isn't rushing to fill space, he's choosing exactly the right words to say based on the conversation or the question he's asked.

People don't remember what you said, they remember how they felt when they said it to you.

Questions for Reflection

- When was the last time I interrupted someone—and why did I feel the need to?

- Who in my life makes me feel deeply heard? How do they do it?

- What opportunities have I missed because I was too focused on talking instead of listening?

- How would my relationships change if I made listening my *default*?

YOU ARE WHO YOU HANG OUT WITH

This is probably one you've heard before, and I'm not pretending I invented it. It's old, overused, and repeated for a reason, because it's been proven true over and over again.

Growing up, I constantly heard, "You're the average of the five people you spend the most time with." I brushed it off as something people just said and didn't think about what it meant in terms of how you live your life. As I got older, I realized it's not fluff at all, it's math.

You don't notice it right away, but your circle is always shaping you, either pulling you forward or anchoring you to who you used to be. One friend skips the gym and suddenly skipping feels justified. Another constantly complains about money and it starts to feel normal to do the same. Someone says you're not supposed to talk about money at all, so you adopt that rule without ever questioning where it came from. Another friend focuses on what they don't have, why they can't succeed, or how the system is stacked against them, and before you know it, that mindset feels familiar.

None of it feels toxic in the moment. It just feels comfortable. Familiar. Like, *if everyone else is doing it, why shouldn't I?*

That realization led me to a simple but uncomfortable question I started asking in my late twenties. When I look at someone in my life, whether a friend, family member, or partner, I ask myself: *Does this person make me better?*

I remember the point when it hit me that I was spending time with people in college that weren't making me a better person. They weren't bad people, they just weren't pushing me. They generally talked about the same things every day, said the same complaints with a victim mindset, the same goals that never actually were accomplished because they weren't serious people.

Then I met someone operating on a completely different level. They were hungry, disciplined, and excited about life. Being around them made me uncomfortable in the best way. It forced a thought I couldn't ignore: *I've been coasting.*

That was the shift. I started craving that kind of energy. I wanted to be around people who talked about ideas instead of gossip, who wanted to build instead of blame, who celebrated wins instead of quietly competing with them.

Once you experience that kind of environment, it's hard to go back.

No one becomes exceptional surrounded by people who are fine being average.

If you want to level up, you can't keep spending most of your time with people who complain about their paychecks, blame their circumstances, or wear mediocrity like a badge of honor. That energy rubs off. It becomes normal. Eventually, it becomes yours.

You don't level up by hoping your friends will come with you. You level up by putting yourself around people who are already there, or relentlessly chasing it themselves.

There's a reason the saying exists: one bad apple spoils the bunch. One good apple doesn't magically fix the rest. If your circle is full of negativity, excuses, jealousy, or complacency, that rot spreads whether you notice it or not.

Your Circle Is Either a Ladder or a Ceiling

Want to get fit? Spend time with people who prioritize health. Gym time becomes social time. Eating clean feels normal. Late nights get replaced with early lifts, and it doesn't feel like a sacrifice.

Want to grow in business or your career? Find mentors. Ask the most successful person in the room for coffee. Listen more than you speak. Pause before responding. Ear hustle what they say and apply it. Your standards rise. Your thinking expands. Average stops feeling acceptable.

Want to improve your mindset, relationships, or spirituality? Spend time with people who live those values.

You don't have to cut everyone off. But you *do* need to audit who has access to your time, your attention, and your influence, because whether you like it or not, you're becoming more like them every day.

Questions for Reflection

- Who in my life consistently brings out the best in me? Who keeps me anchored to my worst habits?
- If I took a week to only hang out with my most driven, healthy, and positive friends, how would I feel?
- What do the people closest to me value most? Are those values aligned with the life I want to live?
- If I keep spending time with my current circle, where will I be five years from now?

BE ENDLESSLY CURIOUS

Your foundation in life is built on what you know and what you've lived through. Every win, failure, mistake, and lesson becomes a tool if you stay curious long enough to learn from it.

Curiosity is what keeps you growing when motivation fades. It's what turns experience into leverage instead of regret. The people who move ahead aren't always the most talented, they're the ones who never stop asking questions.

The Compounding Effect of Learning

Everything in life gets easier when you invest in learning, especially when you apply what you learn in the real world.

This isn't about school or grades. It's about practical education, the kind that never really ends. Every book you read, every conversation you lean into, every risk you take, and every mistake you survive adds another layer to who you are.

The compounding effect here is massive. Read consistently and your thinking sharpens. Pay attention long enough and patterns start to emerge. Over time, you don't just know more, you see more. That's how judgment improves.

You don't become dangerous because you're the smartest person in the room. You become dangerous because you've seen enough, tried enough, and failed enough to understand what actually works.

Curiosity Requires Action

Curiosity isn't collecting information. It's testing it.

You can read about leadership, but you learn it when you have to lead. You can study investing, but you understand it when your own money is involved. You can watch content about relationships, but growth happens when you navigate conflict, communication, and compromise yourself.

The people who stall aren't lazy, they're passive. They consume endlessly without applying anything. Curiosity only compounds when it's paired with action.

The Learning Revolution You're Living In

We're living in the most resource-rich era in human history, and most people barely take advantage of it.

Learning is no longer locked behind textbooks, gatekeepers, or expensive degrees. You don't need permission to get smarter. The smartest person in the room isn't the one with the most credentials, it's the one who knows how to ask the right questions and where to look for answers.

The internet flipped the learning model on its head. You can teach yourself almost anything, anytime, often for free. And now with AI, you don't even have to go searching, you can just ask. If you're not using these tools, you're leaving leverage on the table.

How I Use Curiosity in Real Life

I've learned more about personal finance, investing, negotiation, and career strategy from YouTube than I ever did in a classroom. Channels like Graham Stephan, Andrei Jikh, Chris Williamson, Tae Kim, or Alex Hormozi made concepts click because they were grounded in real decisions and thought execution, not just theory.

With AI, I've helped my dad map out a retirement plan and helped friends build investment strategies in under thirty minutes. We structured Roth IRAs, explored tax considerations, and modeled long-term growth. What once required hours of research or thousands paid to advisors is now accessible to anyone willing to ask better questions.

I use AI tools daily in my sales career too, from writing emails and practicing objection handling to refining pitches and cleaning up data. Not to replace thinking, but to accelerate it. It's like having an assistant, strategist, and tutor in one place.

Learn How to Ask Better Questions

The future doesn't belong to people who know everything. It belongs to people who know how to ask good questions.

Being "prompt-savvy" isn't about being technical, it's about being clear. Give context. Give constraints. Assign a role. Instead of vague questions, frame things intentionally, like asking an AI to act as a financial advisor and build a plan to get out of debt, or act as a hiring manager and critique a resume.

Need to learn about taxes? There are hundreds of CPA-run YouTube channels breaking it down for employees, freelancers, and business owners. Want to improve your resume or cover letter? AI tools can help you refine it quickly, just don't let them replace your voice entirely. They're best used to start the process, not finish it.

Trying to start a business? You can explore niche ideas, pricing models, marketing copy, and outreach strategies in hours instead of months. And if you're a visual learner, platforms like YouTube, Udemy, Coursera, and Skillshare cover almost every skill imaginable at little or no cost.

Stay a Student

You don't need to be a tech genius. You don't need perfect timing. You don't need to know it all. You just need to stay curious enough to keep learning.

The moment you stop being curious is the moment you stop growing. Curiosity keeps you adaptable. It keeps you humble. It keeps you engaged with the world instead of stuck reacting to it.

Because right now, the best knowledge in the world is one well-phrased question away, and curiosity is the key that unlocks it.

Questions for Reflection

- What's something I wish I had learned five years earlier—and what's stopping me from learning it now?

- Am I consuming more *entertainment* or *education* each day?

- What prompt-based tools could help me automate or accelerate my goals right now?

NEVER STOP DREAMING

I went back and forth on how to write this lesson because not everyone will agree with it, and that's fine. But I've watched this exact thing quietly take over too many lives to ignore it.

Never stop dreaming sounds simple, almost cliché, until you realize how rare it becomes as people get older.

When you're in high school or your early twenties, dreaming is easy. You're ambitious, hungry, and mostly unaware of how hard life can hit. Then real life shows up. You get a job. Start making some money. Maybe find a long-term partner. Maybe save for a house. These are real accomplishments, things you should be proud of, moments where you pause and think, *How could it get better than this?*

And slowly, without realizing it, curiosity gets traded for comfort.

There's nothing wrong with being comfortable. Hitting certain milestones, like a solid income, a home, a family, those are meaningful goals. The danger is when comfort turns into coasting.

People reach a place where things are "good enough" and then run the same loop for the next forty years without ever asking what else is possible.

It doesn't happen overnight, in fact it's very subtle. You stop chasing what lights you up. You stop asking what's next. Life becomes wake up, go to class or work, maybe a hobby or two, sleep, repeat. That might describe most people, but that doesn't make it right.

Complacency is the enemy of greatness. The second you stop dreaming, you start decaying. Just because things are stable doesn't mean you stop imagining what more could look like.

I've caught myself slipping into it too. When income is good, relationships are solid, and life feels predictable, it's easy to relax and let the hamster wheel keep spinning. But the moment you lose the internal spark that got you there in the first place is the moment future greatness stops coming out of you.

Success Is Not a Finish Line

This lesson isn't about blind ambition or not being appreciative of how far we've come in our own journey. It's about keeping your soul awake. It's about continuing to grow, not just physically or financially, but emotionally, spiritually, and energetically.

Jesse Itzler is a great example of this. If you don't know who he is, look him up. He started as a white rapper trying to break into music, failed multiple times, pivoted, and eventually co-founded

Marquis Jet, selling it to Warren Buffett and Berkshire Hathaway for an absurd amount of money. The point isn't the money. The point is that he never stopped dreaming and when something didn't work he pivoted until it did.

Even after massive success, he kept pushing, experimenting, creating, and squeezing every ounce out of life. Because the bus of life doesn't slow down just because you're doing okay. It keeps moving through highs and lows either way.

Dreaming doesn't have to mean Lamborghinis or penthouses, unless that's your thing. It could be writing a book, starting a nonprofit, learning to surf, moving to another country, or raising kids differently than you were raised. Whatever your dream is, don't let the muscle atrophy.

The people who stop dreaming are the ones who wake up one day asking, *What happened?*

Dreams give life direction. Goals give dreams structure. Action gives dreams life.

My Personal Vision

For me, it's a lakefront house with boats, four dogs, two jet skis, and a wife I can't wait to come home to, and a couple of kids to raise and bring joy to the world . And once that's built, why not a vineyard?

That's my ladder. Yours doesn't have to look anything like mine. But you better have one, because there are no respawns. No second runs.

You don't want your story to end with *I should've* and you definitely don't want to start out your life story with I took the easy way. You want to look back in fifty years and say, *Hell yes.*

Questions for Reflection

- When was the last time I felt genuinely excited about the future?

- What's a dream I've buried because it felt "unrealistic"—and what's stopping me from revisiting it now?

- What's my version of the lake house, the dream life?

- If nothing held me back—no fear, no judgment, no limits—what would I chase today?

LOVE

DATE YOURSELF FIRST

Let's start with a reality check.

You don't need to be in a relationship to have a good life.

There's an unspoken pressure, especially in your twenties, to have everything figured out. You go to college, graduate, land a job, get into a relationship, and then follow this invisible, pre-approved timeline that says marriage, house, kids, repeat. Somewhere along the way, everyone agreed this was the script.

And if you're not on it, or not hitting milestones "on time," it starts to mess with you. You feel behind. Like something's wrong. Like everyone else got the memo and you didn't.

Here's the truth most people don't want to admit: being single can be one of the most powerful phases of your life if you let it be.

Date yourself First

Learn to stand on your own before inviting someone else in. You cannot have a successful relationship until you find yourself first. In your teens and twenties and even thirties I think this is hard to see unless you were raised in a strong family that focused on self improvement and preservation.

I certainly wasn't, I chased the feeling of being in love for a long time. In some ways I think I craved any kind of stability that would offset a broken household. You could call me a hopeless romantic at the time. After being crushed by a breakup many times I realized the problem is what I'm chasing to begin with. I can't expect to have a strong relationship where some person will come in and fill the gaps of everything I don't have in my own life. Eventually I flipped the narrative and started to date myself first.

Now what the heck does that mean? Date yourself?

It's the conscious decision to spend time alone with your own well being and prioritizing your own happiness. Figure out what energizes you if no one in the world was there to see you or do it for you. Cook your favorite meal alone, Go to a movie by yourself, Go on a hike, Visit a Museum, sit with your thoughts. Just get out and do something and be comfortable in your own skin doing things for yourself before you accept others doing them with you.

When you get comfortable being with yourself, something changes. Dating becomes clearer. You recognize faster who's good for you and who isn't. You stop clinging to potential. You stop fearing loneliness because you already know your own company is enough.

There's nothing wrong with relationships. Hell, love is one of the greatest experiences in life. But too many people get into relationships because they're afraid of being alone. Because they're uncomfortable sitting with themselves. Because society taught them that happiness only counts if you're sharing it with someone else.

When you date yourself first, you attract better people. You build a life you're proud of before asking someone else to share it. And when you do meet someone worth committing to, you show up whole, not broken. You offer love, not neediness.

That's the kind of relationship that lasts.

Questions for Reflection

- Am I afraid of being alone—or excited to spend time with myself?
- What have I learned about myself during periods of solitude?
- What does my dream life look like—and am I building it now, with or without a partner?
- Do I feel like I *need* someone to feel whole—or do I want someone to share my already-whole life with?

ARE THEY "THE ONE"? IS THERE EVEN A "ONE"?

"The one" isn't about perfection. It's about alignment, timing, effort, and a mutual willingness to build something real with another imperfect human being.

The Big Question We All Ask

This is one of those heavy questions that quietly follows most of us around: *How do I know if someone is the one?* And the honest answer is uncomfortable. Most of the time, you don't know, at least not right away.

People love to say, "When you know, you know," but that's movie-script logic. Real life is messier. Real love is built slowly. It's timing, communication, maturity, commitment, and effort layered on top of each other over time. And just as importantly, it's about who *you* are in the relationship, not just who they are.

I've wrestled with this question more times than I can count. I've been in relationships I thought would last forever, relationships I assumed would stay in that honeymoon phase indefinitely. I've also found myself sitting in perfectly "fine" relationships asking, *Is this it?* Not because something was wrong, but because it didn't feel like the fireworks I thought love was supposed to feel like.

After enough failed relationships, some because of me, others because of timing or emotional readiness on both sides, I finally realized I was asking the wrong question. It wasn't just *Are they the one?* It was *Am I capable of being someone else's one?*

What Being "The One" Actually Means

Being "the one" isn't a title someone earns because the stars align or because the first date feels magical. It's not unicorns, fate, or some cosmic moment where everything suddenly makes sense.

It's readiness.

It's the point where you're willing to show up consistently, communicate honestly, and put in the work required for a long-term, emotionally available relationship. It's choosing effort over fantasy.

I spent years chasing that magical feeling, hoping it would carry the relationship when things got hard. Looking back, I can see how much Disney movies and romantic comedies shaped that expectation, teaching us that love should always feel intense, effortless, and exciting. That mindset sets people up for disappointment, because real love doesn't live in constant adrenaline.

It lives in stability, patience, and growth.

On Being Ready

Here's the part people avoid: the best partner in the world won't save a relationship if you're not in the right place yourself.

You have to be grounded on your own. You can't expect someone else to complete you or fix what you haven't addressed. That's not love, that's dependency wearing a nicer label.

Some questions worth sitting with honestly:

- Am I ready to focus on one person and give them what they deserve?
- Do I know my values, my goals, and the kind of life I want to build?
- Am I looking for love, or am I just uncomfortable being alone?
- When I look at my life, am I proud of how I'm showing up?

Only when you have clarity and confidence in yourself can you really evaluate whether someone else is worth building a future with.

Love Versus the Fantasy of Love

Love isn't just butterflies and excitement. It's how you show up when things are boring, messy, inconvenient, or uncomfortable.

You know it's real when:

- You admire who they are, not just how they make you feel.

- You care about their well-being even when it costs you something.

- You're willing to grow, compromise, and stay when it would be easier to leave.

- You don't need them to survive, but you choose them anyway.

It's not about having identical interests or never disagreeing. It's about looking at someone and knowing you'd build a life with them, face setbacks together, chase dreams, fail, rebuild, and keep choosing each other through it all.

That's what "the one" really means.

Questions for Reflection

- Am I emotionally ready to give love—not just receive it?

- What core values do I *need* in a lifelong partner?

- Am I staying because it's right—or because I'm scared of starting over?

- Do I feel inspired, safe, and at peace around this person?

- If I had to choose this person again—with everything I know now—would I?

THE MOST IMPORTANT DECISION OF YOUR LIFE IS WHO YOU MARRY

Who you marry is the single most important decision of your life, not because it's romantic, but because it's practical. Your partner will influence your personal growth, mental health, financial trajectory, parenting style, daily mood, and long-term happiness more than any other single choice you make, so you have to choose intentionally, not emotionally, not impulsively, not out of fear.

The Decision That Changes Everything

It still blows my mind how many people spend more time planning a perfect couple vacation than evaluating long-term compatibility with someone. You'll research flights for weeks, compare hotels, read reviews, build an itinerary, meanwhile you see the same person rush into a relationship, or stay in one, simply because starting over feels exhausting.

We're sold the fantasy that marriage is the finish line, like once you find "the one," the work is done. In reality, it's the beginning. Who you choose as your life partner will either amplify your potential or drain it slowly, day by day, year by year, decision by decision.

If you're with someone who supports your dreams, helps regulate your emotions, challenges you to grow, and brings peace into your life, that's rare, protect it. If you're constantly in conflict, hiding parts of yourself, walking on eggshells, or shrinking to keep the peace, that's not love, that's survival.

Don't spend your life surviving someone else's presence. You should feel seen, safe, and inspired, not just "not alone."

A Simple Truth Successful People Understand

A lot of highly successful people will tell you the same thing in different words, the best decision they ever made wasn't a deal, a job, or a lucky break, it was choosing the right spouse. Not because their partner did the work for them, but because the right partnership becomes a foundation, it gives you stability when life gets chaotic, it gives you honest feedback when your ego flares up, it gives you someone who believes in you when you're doubting yourself.

That's the kind of relationship that becomes a launchpad, not a limitation.

Whether you want to build a business, travel the world, raise a family, or simply live with peace in your home, your partner should be an ally, not an anchor.

What to Look For

This isn't about finding perfection. Everyone comes with baggage. Some people carry trust issues from abandonment or past relationships, some have financial chaos like gambling or uncontrolled debt, some have learned beliefs from family, culture, or religion that shape how they handle love, conflict, and responsibility, and those can be the trickiest because they feel "normal" to the person living them.

The real question isn't, "Do they have flaws?" The question is, "Can we handle each other's flaws with honesty, maturity, and real effort, and still choose each other long-term?"

You don't need someone who completes you. You need someone who complements you, someone who adds value, shares values, and makes the hard parts of life lighter just by being on your team.

This is about alignment, morals, direction, family, finances, lifestyle, faith, health, conflict style, and family planning goals. Love alone isn't enough if the foundation is mismatched. Marry someone you'd want to do life with on a random Tuesday when nothing exciting is happening, not just someone you have fun with on weekends.

The Conversation Most Couples Avoid

The only way I've found to get real clarity is to sit down, turn off your phone, grab a whiteboard or a piece of paper, and let the truth come out. Be fully present, talk through what each of you wants, what you expect, what you're afraid of, what you refuse to tolerate, what kind of life you're trying to build, then compare the two pictures.

If the paths don't line up, don't pretend love will magically solve it. Ask the real questions, where is there flexibility, what compromises are actually possible, what's the long-term outcome of those compromises, and is what you're giving up worth it, or will you resent it five years from now.

And you have to accept this too, it's okay to have hard boundaries, it's okay to say, "I can't do life that way," because you can't go backwards once you build a marriage, a home, a family, a life.

This choice touches everything. Choose with your eyes open.

Questions for Reflection

- How does this relationship impact my energy, purpose, and overall trajectory?

- Can I see this person growing with me for decades, or holding me back out of fear or comfort?

- If everything in life got harder tomorrow, would I still choose this person to walk through it with me?

- Are our values aligned in the key areas: morals, direction, family, finances, lifestyle, faith, health, family planning goals, religion and values.

LOVE HAS LIMITS

Most love is conditional, and that's not a bad thing. Knowing where your boundaries are isn't cold or unromantic, it's necessary. Real love includes limits, and those limits protect your peace, your identity, and your future.

The Lesson I Learned at Nineteen

I learned this the hard way when I was nineteen.

At that age, when someone says, "I love you," your instinct is to melt. You think: *Wow, this person really sees me. They care deeply. This could be it*. You start imagining a future. You overlook red flags. You give them your full trust.

But love, especially young love can be incredibly manipulative if you're not careful. Sometimes people *believe* they love you, until you stop doing what they want. Then suddenly that "love" disappears. Or worse, it turns into a weapon.

In my own experience, I was in a relationship where everything seemed perfect at first. We said all the right things. *"You're my person." "We're forever."* That kind of thing. But over time, reality began to show. She started using love as leverage.

"I do all this for you, and you can't even do this one thing for me?"

"If you really loved me, you'd..."

It slowly chipped away at me. I started realizing that the love wasn't unconditional. It was dependent on how well I played the role she had scripted in her head. She cheated. She lied. She belittled me behind my back.

And yet, she'd still say, *"But I love you."*

What she really meant was, *"I love you when you serve me."*

That's not real love, that's ego with a mask on.

Love Versus Tolerance

The phrase "unconditional love" gets thrown around like it's the highest ideal. But every relationship has conditions, whether people admit it or not.

Here's the difference that matters. Love says, "I care about you deeply." Tolerance says, "I'll accept anything you do, even if it destroys me."

Those are not the same thing.

If someone consistently violates your boundaries, ignores your emotional needs, or takes advantage of your loyalty, walking away isn't weakness, it's strength. It's proof that you've grown enough to value yourself more than the comfort of staying.

You are allowed to say:

- "I love you, but I can't continue this."
- "I forgive you, but I'm choosing something healthier."
- "This doesn't make you a bad person, but it's not the life I want."

Forgiveness is internal. Boundaries are external. You can release resentment without giving someone continued access to hurt you.

That's what healthy love looks like. Not limitless tolerance, but mutual respect, accountability, and care that doesn't require you to lose yourself in the process.

Questions for Reflection

- Have I tolerated pain or disrespect in the name of "love"?
- What specific behaviors are deal-breakers for me—and am I honoring that?
- Do I confuse forgiveness with permission?
- What does healthy love with boundaries look like to me?

JUST END IT IF IT'S NOT RIGHT

I f you keep asking yourself whether you should stay, you probably already have your answer. Don't overthink what your gut has been telling you for a while. If it's not right, just end it.

The Courage to Walk Away

Here's a truth we don't say out loud enough: breaking up takes courage. It doesn't make you cold. It doesn't mean you didn't care. It means you're honest enough to admit that something isn't working before it turns toxic or slowly drains the life out of you.

Most people wait too long to learn this. I know I did.

I stayed in relationships far longer than I should have, not because they were great, but because they were *almost* what I wanted. They had eighty percent of what I was looking for, but that missing twenty percent gnawed at me constantly. On paper, everything checked out. In real life, I wasn't excited to see them after a long day. I loved the idea of the relationship more than the reality of being in it.

No one is perfect, but that doesn't mean you're supposed to settle either.

The Excuses We Make

A lot of people stay because they don't want to be the bad guy. They tell themselves:

- "I don't want to hurt them."
- "They're so good to me, I should be happy."
- "Maybe I'm the problem."
- "What if I don't find someone better?"

So instead of having the hard conversation, they emotionally check out but stay physically present. They grow distant. Passive-aggressive. Detached. Sometimes they flirt with other people, hoping the other person will end it first so they don't have to carry the guilt.

Don't do that.

If you know it's not going to work, be the one who ends it cleanly and honestly. Rip the band-aid off. It will hurt in the moment, but it's far better than dragging someone through slow, confusing emotional damage just to avoid discomfort. Ten minutes of hatred and anger from the other person is better than years of being unsure and miserable.

The Stress Test

If you're unsure, ask yourself a few honest questions, and don't rationalize your answers away.

Do I enjoy doing absolutely nothing with this person? If silence feels heavy, irritating, or awkward, that matters.

If we broke up today, would I feel sad or relieved? If relief shows up first, listen to it.

If I saw them with someone else next week, would I truly care? If the answer is no, or even "not really," you're already gone emotionally.

The longer you avoid the truth, the messier it becomes.

An Act of Self-Respect

At its core, this lesson isn't just about them. It's about you. Your peace. Your future. Your self-respect.

Ending something that isn't right is an act of honesty, not failure. You should give yourself credit for being in the relationship at all. You showed up. You tried. You cared. That counts.

But if your gut keeps whispering that this isn't it, don't drown it out with excuses. Listen. Have the conversation. End it with kindness and clarity.

Staying in the wrong relationship costs you time you'll never get back. The right relationship won't require you to constantly convince yourself to stay.

Questions for Reflection

- What am I really afraid of? Is it hurting them, or being alone?
- Have I already emotionally checked out of the relationship?
- Is staying helping us grow, or just postponing the inevitable?
- Am I proud of how I'm showing up in this relationship?
- What would my future self thank me for: staying or leaving?

HOW TO DEAL WITH MODERN DATING

Modern dating has become such a weird web of complexity. Society has pushed the thought of women being independent, supporting themselves and choosing men that are emotionally unavailable, broken and mysterious. In the notebook Allie chooses Noah, the deeply emotional man who's poor and unpredictable instead of the stable fiance she already had. Why?

If a man says hi, here I am, women are trained to think ok what's wrong with this guy. Versus the guy who plays hard to get, is emotionally immature, and aloof about who he pursues.

Chris Williamson from the Modern Wisdom Podcast speaks about this concept in that it has become this way because we've been taught in general that things are only worth getting if they are hard to get to begin with. If the guy or girl is super into me then why would I be interested in them instead of putting that selfish thought aside and taking into consideration the person who is actually in front of you. When you add technology and dopamine hits to that already complicated mindset, you can start to understand why global birth rates are declining, why people are getting married later in life and why staying in a committed relationship has become the harder choice vs leaving and going back on "the apps"

Dating apps like Hinge, Bumble, Tinder, etc. and digital communication have fundamentally changed how relationships begin and develop. Success in modern dating often requires understanding both the psychology of online connection and maintaining authentic human interaction skills.

The New Reality of Finding Love

According to Forbes 53% of people under the age of 30 have used dating apps/sites to find love in 2025..Most people in our generation meet through apps, social media, or online platforms. The days of meeting your future spouse at the grocery store or through mutual friends haven't disappeared entirely, but they're no longer the norm. This shift requires new skills and mindsets that our parents never needed.

Dating apps are designed to be addictive, instead of effective at creating lasting relationships. Understanding this changes how you use them.

Too many options can actually decrease satisfaction and increase anxiety. Having endless potential matches makes people less likely to invest deeply in getting to know any single person.

Just like social media, dating profiles show curated versions of people's lives. Someone's most attractive photos, best jokes, and most interesting hobbies. This creates unrealistic expectations and disappointment when reality doesn't match the profile.

Me personally? I've been on many many dates that started from an app swipe or like. Some turning into great longterm relationships in which I personally grew from and became a better more well rounded man because of. Much like you reading this I've also had the worst dates and failures pursuing a relationship from dating apps as well.

Back when I had moved back in with my mother after graduating college and breaking up with my college sweetheart I had decided to try online dating after one of my friends pushed me to try it after he met his fiance on bumble. So I downloaded the app and started swiping. After a few days I had some matches and started conversing with one particular person. She seemed nice enough and her pictures made her look drop dead gorgeous so after a day of communicating I asked if she wanted to go on a date. She accepted and said to meet her at her and her roommate's apartment before heading out to dinner. I said ok great, told my mom I was going on a date and that I'd be back later. I drove 30 mins to downtown Atlanta up to a super nice apartment complex. I texted her that I was there and she told me to come up to her apartment and gave me the apartment number. I walked into the building and after walking around what felt like a maze, got to her apartment door. I knocked, no one answered. I thought ok maybe they are playing music or on the balcony so I tried to gently turn the door handle. Locked. I then got a phone call from this girl asking if I was there. I said yes I'm outside your front door and she said ok before you come in I need to tell you something. I froze... here I am standing in an apartment complex with my first experience on a dating app and she said I need to tell you something first? I said ok what? Thinking she was going to bail.

She responds that the girl in the pictures isn't me. I got Catfished...

I used to see episodes of the show catfished that was popular in the early 2000's but never in my wildest dreams did I think this would happen to me.

I naively responded ok why would you use someone else's pictures. What do you look like? She said that's my best friend...

I immediately hung up the phone and made a dash for the exit. In the heat of the moment thinking what the heck was that, I couldn't figure out where the front door of the apartment complex was so I went out through the emergency exit in the gym and made the alarm go off. Blocked her number and drove back home feeling like dating apps are a scam. I walked back into my moms house and she said wow you're home early. I told her what had transpired and she lost it laughing hysterically saying that's why you don't meet people on the internet as many baby boomers used to think. We still laugh about it to this day.

My point being is in a world where modern dating has made it easy to meet someone and have multiple dates a week or even a day. Be cautious with online interactions and think about what you want in a partner longterm, and don't be so quick to judge the guy who comes up to talk to you or the girl who smiles at you wanting you to go say something to her. That person could end up being the best possible thing that ever happened.

With this goal in mind I thought it would be good to lay out some strategies below that could help one navigate modern dating.

Strategies That Actually Work

1. Quality Over Quantity

More options don't lead to better outcomes, they usually lead to burnout. Limit yourself to two or three apps max so you're not overwhelmed or half-invested everywhere. Spend more time on thoughtful messages instead of mass-swiping, and set daily time limits so you don't fall into endless scrolling disguised as "trying."

2. Optimize Your Profile Without Pretending

Use recent photos that actually look like you. Include variety, a close-up, a full-body shot, and a few photos doing things you genuinely enjoy. Your bio should give people something to respond to, not just a list of traits. Let your personality show, whether that's humor, honesty, or what you're genuinely looking for. The goal isn't to attract everyone, it's to attract the right people.

3. Move Beyond the App Quickly

Don't spend weeks messaging someone you've never met. There are tens of millions of people in your age range in the U.S. alone, there will be other matches. Guys, ask her out. Ladies, be open to giving a guy a real shot. FaceTime or video calls are a great middle step to build comfort and avoid surprises. Keep early dates simple and public, coffee, lunch, or my personal favorite, tacos.

4. Manage Digital Communication Like an Adult

Response time doesn't equal interest, people have lives. Use voice notes or calls to add tone and personality that text can't carry. Be clear about your communication style and boundaries early. And don't try to build an entire relationship through texting alone, it's a tool, not a foundation.

Red Flags in Digital Dating

Just like in face-to-face relationships, red flags exist in digital dating, they just show up differently. The first place to pay attention is someone's profile. If every photo is a group picture and you can't tell who the person actually is, that's worth noting. The same goes for profiles filled with heavy filters or overly polished, professional shots. Putting your best foot forward is normal, but authenticity matters more. Most people aren't walking around photo-ready all day, and profiles that feel overly curated often hide something real.

Next, look at what the profile is actually saying, or not saying. Does the information feel contradictory or too good to be true? Is it vague to the point of meaning nothing, or completely empty altogether? On the flip side, does it overshare or lean into explicit content right away? None of these are automatic dealbreakers on their own, but together they tell a story. You're looking for a balance between openness and self-awareness, not mystery for mystery's sake and not a résumé of exaggerated claims.

The way someone communicates matters even more than how their profile looks. A major red flag is refusing to video chat or meet in person after a reasonable amount of time, especially if excuses keep stacking up. Another is pressure, whether that's pushing for personal details, location information, or intimate photos before trust is established. Love-bombing is another common trap in digital dating, when someone moves extremely fast emotionally, using intensity to create a false sense of connection before anything real has been built.

Pay attention to consistency. Someone who constantly cancels or reschedules plans without effort to follow through is showing you their priorities. The same goes for people who only message late at night or only when it's convenient for them. These patterns usually aren't accidental, and they tend to become more pronounced over time, not less.

Red flags aren't about judging someone harshly or assuming the worst. They're about protecting your time, energy, and emotional well-being. The earlier you notice them, the easier it is to step away without over-investing. Digital dating moves fast, but that doesn't mean you have to ignore your instincts to keep up.

Questions for Reflection

- How do my dating app habits reflect my actual relationship goals?

- Am I using digital dating as a complement to or replacement for developing real-world social skills?

- What patterns do I notice in my digital dating experiences, both positive and negative?

- How can I maintain authenticity while presenting my best self online?

- What boundaries do I need to set around digital dating to protect my mental health?

PART III

FAMILY

CHERISH YOUR PARENTS BEFORE THEY'RE GONE

You only get one set of parents. Don't wait until it's too late to appreciate them.

When you're young, your parents feel permanent. They're just there. Your safety net. Your support system. The people you assume will always answer the phone, always show up, always be in the background of your life. Even when they annoy you or push your buttons, you never really question their presence.

Then time starts to move.

You get older. They get older. And without some dramatic moment or clear warning, things begin to change.

For me, it was the small things that hit the hardest. Repeated stories. Slower steps. More doctor appointments. Less energy. More gray hair. Somewhere along the way, I realized they weren't invincible anymore. They weren't the unshakable adults I grew up believing they were. And just as quietly, the roles began to shift. I wasn't the kid who needed protecting. I was the adult who needed to truly see them, not just as my parents, but as people who had given most of their lives to raising someone else.

The Regret I Don't Want You to Have

I've had friends lose their parents suddenly. No warning. No final conversation. No last hug. No chance to say, "I love you," one more time. And every single time, the regret sounded the same.

"I thought I had more time."

They didn't regret not working harder. They didn't regret not making more money. They regretted not calling back. Not visiting more. Not listening closely enough. Not asking the questions they always assumed they could ask later.

That reality changed how I show up with my own parents. Once it really sunk in that they wouldn't be around forever, I started calling them every day. Not always for long conversations. Sometimes just to check in, to say hey, to ask how their day was. I made a quiet decision that I wasn't going to carry the regret of wishing I'd done more.

That small shift meant more than I realized. To them, it was just a phone call. To me, it was validation and a small thank you for being my parents.

Even if your parents are overbearing, too involved, distant, or hard to connect with at times, they're still yours. You'll never get another set of people who know your entire story from the beginning, who loved you before you had anything to offer, who rooted for you when you didn't even know who you were yet.

They changed your diapers. Stayed up all night when you were sick. Sat through awkward school performances. Held you through bad breakups. Watched you make mistakes and still loved you anyway. They gave you what they had, whether it was a lot or just enough, whether they did it perfectly or imperfectly.

Your life doesn't have to revolve around them. You're allowed to grow, set boundaries, and live your own story. That's part of becoming an adult. But within all of that, cherish them. Call more often. Visit when you can. Ask about their past. Listen to the stories, even if you've heard them before.

One day, the things that feel ordinary now will feel priceless. And you'll wish you could hear their voice just one more time.

Questions for Reflection

- When was the last time I thanked my parents—not for something specific, but just for being in my life?

- If tomorrow was the last day I could speak to one of them, what would I want to say?

- Do I know my parents beyond them being Mom and Dad in my life? Do I know who they were before me?

DON'T LET OTHERS DECIDE IF YOU WANT KIDS

The decision to have children is one of the most personal choices you'll ever make. It shapes your time, your priorities, your values, your identity, and your legacy. Because of that, it should be made on your terms, not out of pressure, expectation, or fear of disappointing someone else.

The Unspoken Pressure

This topic is heavier than most people admit, especially in your twenties and early thirties, when every family gathering starts to feel like a quiet interrogation disguised as small talk.

"Do you want kids?"
"When are you going to settle down?"
"Don't wait too long or you'll regret it."

The questions come from everywhere. Parents. Grandparents. Friends who already have kids. Friends who don't. Society at large. And even when they're asked casually, they carry weight, because they imply there's a correct answer and a timeline you're supposed to follow.

I've had countless conversations about this with friends and family. Some wish they had waited longer before having children. Others regret not having them at all. Neither side is wrong. Both are speaking from emotion, identity, and lived experience. And both reinforce the same truth: no one else can make this decision for you.

For a long time, I didn't want kids at all. In my early twenties, I couldn't picture marriage either. I valued freedom, flexibility, and the ability to chase my goals without restriction. The idea of settling down felt like giving something up. As I got older, that perspective shifted. I started thinking maybe, if I met the right person, if it made financial sense, if life felt stable enough, then I'd consider it. And now, looking ahead, I want kids more than ever. I can't wait to be a dad someday. What changed wasn't pressure or age, it was clarity. My values evolved, my priorities matured, and the idea of building something bigger than myself started to matter more than protecting my independence.

That's the point. This decision is allowed to change over time. You don't need to have it figured out early, and you definitely shouldn't rush it to satisfy anyone else's timeline. Maybe you've always assumed you'd be a parent. Maybe you've never wanted kids. Or maybe you're somewhere in the middle, wanting freedom, purpose, and meaning, but unsure whether parenting is the path that gets you there. That uncertainty doesn't mean you're behind or broken. It means you're thinking. Just make sure the choice, whenever it comes, is yours, and that you're making it with the right person, for the right reasons.

Choosing Intentionally, Not Automatically

The worst way to make this decision is by default. Don't do it because it feels like "the next step." Don't do it because your parents want grandchildren. Don't do it because your partner expects it without conversation. And don't avoid it out of fear either.

This decision deserves honesty.

Ask yourself real questions. Do you feel called to raise and guide another human being? Are you willing to sacrifice time, energy, freedom, and comfort for decades, not just during the cute stages? Does the responsibility excite you, even when you think about the hard parts, or does it quietly fill you with dread?

There's no right answer, only a right answer for you.

John Cena once said publicly that he doesn't want children, not because he dislikes kids, but because his curiosity about life and desire to explore everything it has to offer conflicts with the level of presence and commitment he believes good parenting requires. That kind of self-awareness matters. Knowing what you *can* give is just as important as knowing what you want.

Here's a simple litmus test: if no one were watching, no parents, no friends, no social expectations, what would you choose?

Your Life, Your Timeline

You're not behind if you don't have kids by a certain age. You're not selfish if you choose to wait. And you're not incomplete if you decide it's not your path at all.

Parenthood is a massive responsibility. It's also an incredible reward for those who genuinely want it. Both things can be true at the same time.

This is your life. You're the one who has to live it every day. Make decisions based on what you want and what you're capable of giving, not on guilt, pressure, or borrowed expectations. Whatever you choose, choose it consciously, because few decisions shape a life more than this one.

Questions for Reflection

- Have I ever asked myself what I want when it comes to parenthood—without outside influence?

- Do I feel pressure to have kids, or excitement about the possibility?

- What kind of parent would I want to be-and am I prepared to take on that role?

- What does a full life look like to me-with or without children?

- Am I choosing based on fear, love, or alignment with who I am?

YOU DON'T PICK YOUR PARENTS, AND YOUR PARENTS DIDN'T PICK YOU

You don't get to choose your parents. And they didn't get to choose you. What you *do* get to choose is how you handle that relationship, regardless of how it turned out.

Let's be real, at some point everyone has had the thought, *Why didn't my parents do things differently?*

Why didn't they invest earlier, love harder, listen better, protect more, understand you the way you needed? Why were they the way they were?

We all look back and wish our parents had given us more, acted differently, parented better, or seen us more clearly for who we were becoming. That frustration is especially strong in your teens and twenties, when you're forming your own identity and starting to see their flaws more clearly.

You can't change the past. You don't get to swap out your mom or dad. And they didn't get to design you either. Your parents were people long before they were parents. They had their own dreams, heartbreaks, fears, trauma, blind spots, and limitations. They carried beliefs shaped by their upbringing, their culture, their circumstances, and the tools they had at the time. Every choice they made, every mistake, every sacrifice shaped the version of them that showed up for you.

That doesn't mean you excuse pain. It doesn't mean you minimize what hurt you. And it definitely doesn't mean you allow yourself to be walked over.

It means you stop waiting for them to become someone different so you can finally move on.

Healing doesn't come from denial or blame. It comes from acceptance. Accepting that your parents are human. That they tried and failed. That they loved you in the only ways they knew how, maybe too much, maybe not enough. That they were figuring it out in real time, just like you are now.

This lesson goes both ways. As much as you need to accept them for who they are, they need to accept you too. And if they don't? You can still choose peace by choosing growth over resentment.

You can be grateful for what you had, even if it wasn't perfect. You can forgive without forgetting. You can set boundaries and still love them. You can move forward without rewriting a story you didn't author.

What matters now is how *you* show up. What you choose to carry forward. What you choose to put down. What patterns you repeat and which ones you finally end.

Because at the end of the day, you're here. You survived. You grew. And you get to decide how this relationship shapes your life moving forward, not the past.

Questions for Reflection

- What do I wish my parents had done differently—and have I voiced it or just carried it silently?
- Where do I need to accept my parents as flawed humans, not just authority figures?
- Have I been holding on to resentment longer than it's served me?
- What part of my relationship with my parents am I ready to heal—or redefine?
- How would my life change if I stopped waiting for them to be different?

SIBLINGS ARE YOUR FIRST REFLECTION OF YOURSELF

No one will frustrate you more, or understand you better, than your siblings. The tension, rivalry, and shared history you have with them is one of your earliest training grounds for real life.

This is a lesson I didn't fully appreciate until I got older. Your siblings are often your first mirror. They reflect who you are when you're not trying to impress anyone. They see your raw reactions, your insecurities, your ego, and your patterns long before the rest of the world does.

Growing up as the middle child with two brothers, I can tell you it wasn't always fun. There were arguments, power struggles, and days I didn't want to be in the same room as them. Attention felt scarce. Validation felt competitive. It often felt like you had to fight just to be seen.

But mixed into all of that were moments of admiration, learning, and quiet trust. We fought over stupid things, the last slice of pizza, who got more attention, who was "winning" at life that week. And yet, when it actually mattered, there was always an unspoken understanding.

You can annoy me. You can piss me off. But if anyone else messes with you, I've got your back.

That kind of loyalty is rare outside of family, and you don't fully realize its value until you experience the world without it.

The First Classroom for Human Behavior

Siblings give you a crash course in real human interaction long before you have language for it. If you're the oldest, you learn responsibility early, sometimes before you're ready. If you're the youngest, you learn adaptability and how to find your place in someone else's system. And if you're the middle child, like me, you often learn survival, how to carve out an identity without getting overlooked, how to read the room, and how to balance competing personalities.

Those dynamics don't disappear when you grow up. They follow you into friendships, romantic relationships, and work environments. How you handle conflict. How you compete. How you withdraw. How you seek approval. Much of that gets rehearsed with your siblings first.

Brothers and sisters have a way of calling you out that no one else can. They know your buttons. They know your weak spots. They remember who you were before you reinvented yourself. And even when it's uncomfortable, that honesty shapes you.

The Bond That Evolves, Not Disappears

I didn't always appreciate my brothers growing up. I wanted space. I wanted independence. I wanted to be my own person, separate from the family identity. That's normal. Distance is often part of growth.

But as I've gotten older, I've realized how much that relationship shaped me. The patience it demanded. The forgiveness it required. The ability to move past conflict without cutting someone out completely. Even now, the relationship continues to teach me presence and perspective.

You might drift apart from your siblings as life pulls you in different directions. Careers, families, distance. But there's still a tether there, a shared history no one else can replace.

The Shared Foundation

Think about it. Who else knows your embarrassing childhood moments, your weird habits, your awkward teenage phase, and still loves you anyway?

No one will test your emotional regulation quite like a sibling. But no one else will understand your childhood, your parents, your environment, and your early life the way they do either. That shared foundation becomes an anchor in adulthood, something you can return to when life gets chaotic.

Your siblings aren't just part of your past. They're part of how you learned to be human.

Questions for Reflection

- How have my siblings shaped the way I communicate, love, or handle conflict?
- What unresolved tension still lingers between us?
- Can I make space for healing, reconnection, or more honest conversations with them?
- How can I better support my siblings, even if we live separate lives now?

CREATE THE TRADITIONS YOU WISH YOU HAD

Every family runs on traditions, whether they realize it or not, some are intentional, others are accidental, but either way they shape how you experience connection, belonging, and what home feels like over time.

Here's the part most people don't realize until later in life, you don't have to inherit traditions, you can create them.

Growing up, you absorb patterns without ever questioning them, how holidays were handled, how conflict was avoided or confronted, how affection was shown or withheld, what was celebrated and what was ignored, all of it quietly teaches you what "normal" looks like.

For some people that normal felt warm and connected, for others it felt chaotic, distant, or emotionally thin, most people fall somewhere in between.

It's easy to get stuck wishing things had been different, wishing your family talked more, gathered more, handled hard moments better, but adulthood gives you a shift most people never fully step into, you're no longer just a product of your family, you're a builder of what comes next.

Traditions aren't grand gestures or expensive events, they're small, repeatable moments that create consistency, weekly dinners, Sunday phone calls, annual trips, shared meals, simple check-ins, showing up the same way often enough that it becomes expected.

What matters isn't how impressive they look, it's that they exist.

I didn't fully appreciate this until I got older and noticed how easily people drift when no one takes responsibility for keeping connections alive, life gets busy, schedules pull people apart, distance grows quietly, and traditions are how you fight that drift.

You Get to Redefine "Family Time"

Maybe your family never ate together, maybe holidays were stressful instead of joyful, maybe no one talked openly about how they were really doing, you can acknowledge that without staying stuck in it.

Creating new traditions isn't about pretending the past didn't happen, it's about deciding what you want the future to feel like.

You can be the person who suggests the trip, hosts the dinner, makes the call, reaches out consistently, creates space for connection instead of waiting for it to magically appear.

That effort might not always be reciprocated evenly, and that's okay, leadership in families often looks like initiative, not balance.

One day, whether you have a partner, kids, or a chosen family of friends, the traditions you build now will become someone else's baseline, they'll remember how things felt around you, safe, consistent, fun, or rushed, distant, and unpredictable.

You don't need to recreate what you experienced yourself to have a version of family, you just need to be intentional about the environment you help create.

Traditions turn time into memory, and memory into meaning.

Questions for Reflection

- What traditions from your upbringing do you want to keep, and which ones are you ready to replace with something better?

- Where in your family life do you feel disconnection, and what small, repeatable moment could you create to change that?

- If no one else took the lead in your family, what relationship would quietly fade, and are you willing to be the one who shows up anyway?

- When people think back on time spent with you, what do you want them to remember it felt like?

NEVER FORGET WHERE YOU COME FROM

No matter how far you climb or how fast your life changes, never lose touch with where you came from. Your roots aren't something to outgrow or apologize for, they're your foundation, and if you let them be, they're also your fuel.

The Sacred Connection to Your Origin

It's easy to want distance from your past. Some people grow up in small towns they couldn't wait to leave, others come from families that felt limiting, chaotic, or hard to explain. Some of us, like me, come from another country entirely.

I moved to America from Italy when I was a kid, and even at that age I understood there was something sacred about not forgetting where I came from. I've always made a point to stay connected to that part of myself, to honor the culture, the food, the people, and the history that shaped me before I ever had a say in it.

This isn't about romanticizing your past or pretending it was perfect. It's about respecting it. Your origin story shaped how you think, how you communicate, how you show up, and how you see the world. It gave you your edge. That difference isn't something to smooth out, it's your superpower.

Your Story Is Part of Your Identity

In a world where everyone is trying to stand out, the irony is that the most powerful thing you can do is lean into what already makes you different. And that always starts with where you came from.

If you're from a small town, don't downplay it. It taught you humility, grit, and community. If you're from another country, wear that proudly. If your family history is complicated, don't run from it, understand it. Complexity builds depth, and depth builds character.

For me, being Italian-American is something I carry intentionally. I think often about the risk my parents took leaving Italy to move to America, chasing a better life for their kids without knowing exactly how it would turn out. I'm deeply grateful they did, because I wouldn't be where I am today without that decision.

At the same time, I appreciate what they left behind. The long family dinners, sitting at the table for hours while food kept getting passed around. The loud, passionate conversations that looked like full-blown arguments to outsiders, even though we were debating nothing important at all. Those moments shaped how I connect, how I value family, and how I show love.

That's where I come from. And I don't want to forget it.

Because when you stay grounded in your roots, success doesn't hollow you out. It deepens you. It keeps you grateful. It keeps you human. And it reminds you that no matter how far you go, you're standing on something real.

Questions for Reflection

- Where did I come from, and how does foundation shape how I see the world?

- What traditions or values from my upbringing still matter to me today?

- Have I tried to hide or downplay where I'm from to fit in or get ahead?

- In what ways can I honor my past without being held back by it?

PART IV

FITNESS

FITNESS IS THE FOUNDATION FOR FINANCE

Without your health, nothing else in life fully works. It fuels your energy, sharpens your focus, stabilizes your mood, and creates the capacity to show up powerfully in every other domain, love, work, family, ambition, and legacy.

The Fifty-Percent Life I Used to Live

There was a time when I took my health completely for granted. Like a lot of guys in high school, I thought I was invincible. I ate like garbage, skipped workouts, stayed up late, and told myself I'd "lock it in later," as if health was something you schedule once everything else is figured out.

Over time, I realized I was lying to myself.

I was tired all the time. Foggy during the day. I felt like shit, looked like shit, and didn't like what I saw in the mirror. My confidence was low, my patience was thin, and my energy was inconsistent. I thought to myself this can't be normal,I was in high school so I wasn't just busy or stressed, I was operating at maybe fifty percent and calling it life.

That's when I understood something most people don't want to face. Your health isn't one priority among many, it's the base layer everything else is built on. When your health is off, every other part of life becomes harder than it needs to be. When it's solid, everything else has room to grow.

This Isn't About only looking Good

The goal here isn't to be aesthetic or getting shredded. It's about respecting your body as the engine that powers your goals, your presence, and your potential.

You can't fully pursue love, success, stability, or impact if your body is constantly working against you. If you're out of breath walking up stairs. If a short walk with your dog feels exhausting. If you're sick all the time because you don't sleep, your diet is trash, or you treat recovery like an afterthought.

If your energy is off, your mindset will be off. If your sleep is garbage, your attitude will be garbage. If your body feels weak, it becomes harder to think clearly, lead confidently, or show up patiently for the people you care about.

That's not motivational talk, that's reality.

No amount of money, discipline, or ambition will compensate for a weak foundation. You can grind for a while, but eventually your body will call to collect.

Health Is Self-Respect in Action

Taking care of your health is one of the most basic forms of self-respect. It's an acknowledgment to yourself that if you want more out of life, you need the capacity to sustain it.

Before you try to become a better boyfriend or girlfriend, build wealth, lead others, or chase big goals, do yourself a favor and build a strong relationship with your body first. Learn how it responds to movement, rest, good food intake, and consistency. Treat it like something worth protecting. As the Bible says, your body is a temple, and it deserves to be honored as such.

Because when your health improves, your standards rise. Your confidence follows. Your patience expands. And your ability to show up fully stops feeling forced.

Health doesn't guarantee success, but without it, everything else becomes an uphill fight.

And life is hard enough already.

Questions for Reflection

- On a scale from 1–10, how would I rate my physical health right now? Why?

- Am I showing up for my health the way I show up for my job, my family, or my goals?

- What's one simple commitment I can make this week to improve my well-being?

- Where have I been making excuses when it comes to my health? Why?

KEEP MOVING

Movement is one of the most underrated tools for longevity, clarity, and energy. It doesn't have to be intense or impressive, it just has to be consistent.

The Passeggiata Principle

I used to dread going on a walk with my mom after a big meal or dinner. She would always ask "who wants to go on a walk?" I hated it. What's the point?

I used to laugh when I saw people in my neighborhood going for a walk after dinner. No weights, no treadmill, no sprint intervals, just strolling around the block. I'd think, *what's the point of that?*

Now I get it.

They weren't trying to burn calories or hit a step count, they were living in a way that kept movement woven into their day. It wasn't about performance, it was about lifestyle.

In Italy, there's a tradition called the *passeggiata*, a casual walk after dinner, usually around the neighborhood or town square. It's not exercise in the traditional sense. It's for digestion, fresh air, conversation, and presence. It's movement without pressure, and it's baked into daily life.

Contrast that with how most of us live now. Everything is designed for convenience. Drive-thrus. Food Delivery. Screens. Chairs. We've outsourced movement and turned it into something we either schedule aggressively or avoid completely. Somewhere along the way, we lost the idea that moving your body doesn't have to feel like punishment.

Finding Your Movement

As I've gotten older, I've realized that cardio isn't just about burning fat. It's about staying alive longer, feeling better, and thinking clearer. But that doesn't mean it has to be running or spin class. For me, it's sports. I grew up playing soccer, and more recently, I've been obsessed with pickleball. Two or three times a week, I show up to play, sweat, and stay sharp. I burn calories, stay limber, and socialize—three wins in one go.

And that's the whole point. It doesn't have to be boring or robotic. It just has to keep you moving.

Movement is Medicine

Not everyone loves the gym. That's fine. I don't love traditional cardio either. But I do believe everyone needs to move. Walk your dog. Bike to the store. Join a rec league. Take the stairs. Play with your kids. Go for a twenty-minute walk after meals. Dance in your kitchen, if that's your thing.

It's not about a six-pack-it's about having the energy and capability to show up in every area of your life. Do you want to crush it in your job? Move. Do you want to have better mental health? Move. Do you want to be a more present partner or parent? Get up and Move.

The most successful people I know are always moving. Not just physically—but mentally, emotionally, and spiritually. And it often starts with how they treat their body.

You don't have to be the strongest or fastest. You just have to stay active, because the moment you stop moving, everything else starts to slow down with you. Your mind isn't as sharp, your reactions aren't as quick, your body isn't as strong, your mindset isn't as positive.

Questions for Reflection

- What is one way I can incorporate more movement into my daily routine—even if it's not a traditional workout?

- When was the last time I moved my body for joy, not just obligation?

- What form of activity do I enjoy doing (sports, walking, dancing, etc.) and how can I do more of it?

- If I viewed movement as essential to my mental clarity and long-term health—not just weight loss—how would my routine change?

START BIOHACKING EARLY

What is Biohacking?

The technical definition according to our good friend Google is making intentional, data driven changes to your lifestyle, diet, and environment to optimize your physical and mental performance. Think of it as the ultimate combo of science + discipline + optimization.

My definition is trying things that might suck at first in order to improve yourself longterm.

It's about recovery, mental performance, energy, resilience, and longevity. When you start doing it in your twenties and thirties, you separate yourself from 99 percent of people who go their whole lives barely paying attention to modern science and expecting their local doctor to save the day if something goes wrong.

I advise everyone to look up Andrew Huberman and Dr. Rhonda Patrick. They are leading the charge on a lot of biohacking tips and tricks to take into consideration as you create your own personal stack.

Optimize your body and brain before something breaks. Biohacking isn't a luxury—it's the new baseline for people who want to perform well, live longer, and feel better.

The Ice Bath Revelation

I still remember the first time I did both a sauna and cold plunge.

I stepped into the ice bath and thought, "What the hell am I doing?" Every instinct screamed to jump out. After those agonizing few minutes, however, it was like I unlocked a superpower. The alertness, the energy, the mental calm-I felt unbeatable for the rest of the day.

Same with the sauna. My first time sitting in 190°F heat, I was sweating like crazy thinking, "Why would anyone do this to themselves?" Once I stepped out and my body cooled down for 10 minutes I felt clear headed. My sinuses were clear, I felt like damn this is good for me. Looking back, this experience is what led me to start biohacking even though I didn't know that's what I was doing at the time.

My Personal Stack

Here's what I personally use and why:

Cold Therapy (Plunges or Cold Showers)

- My routine: 2–4 minutes, 1-2x/week

- Benefits: Reduces inflammation, boosts mood, sharpens focus, supports fat loss.

I could probably do this one more if I'm being honest with myself.

Sauna (Heat Shock Therapy)

- My routine: 20 minutes, 4–5x/week- usually post-workout.

- Benefits: Triggers heat shock proteins, detoxes the body, improves heart health and endurance.

- Fun fact: Dr. Rhonda Patrick cites Dr. Jari Laukkanen's studies in Finland show that regular sauna use is linked to 50% lower cardiovascular mortality and 40% reduced risk of dementia.

NAD+ (I use RHO)

- My routine: I take it every morning first thing before I have a cup of coffee

- Benefits: NAD+ powers cellular energy and DNA repair. It declines 50% by your forties.

Athletic Greens (AG1)

- My routine: I use one scoop every morning. It covers my daily micronutrients, plus gut health.

- Benefits: It's hard to get 75+ nutrients every day. AG1 makes it easy.

Magnesium

- My routine: I take it every night before sleep for better rest and recovery.

- Benefits: Improves deep sleep, lowers cortisol, supports hormonal balance.

Creatine (5g Each Morning,15g if I didn't sleep the night before)

- My routine: I take it each morning with my NAD+

- Benefits: Enhances both physical and cognitive performance.

Huberman talks about this on his podcast.

Questions for Reflection

- Which tool or habit am I most curious about—and when will I start implementing it?

- Am I living in a way that supports the energy I want to bring to my work, relationships, and future?

- What would my fifty-year-old self thank me for starting today?

DIET IS THE KEY TO EVERYTHING

You can't outwork a bad diet.

What you eat either fuels your goals, or fights them. Nutrition is the foundation your energy, performance, and mental clarity are built on.

Premium Gas

For the longest time, I thought that if I crushed a workout, I earned the right to eat whatever I wanted. Burgers, pizza, Cheesecake -no big deal. I figured I'd just burn it off tomorrow and maybe in my teens and early 20's this might've been the case. As you get into your late twenties, you quickly realize this isn't the case anymore for most of us. This led me to change my mindset about what I was putting in my body much like we consider the kind of gas we put in our cars.

I cleaned things up and focused on protein, whole foods, hydration, and consistency. That's when I noticed my workouts were more productive, my sleep improved, my mood stabilized, and my body finally started to change. Taking mind of what you put into your body is just as important as what you do to workout your body.

Your Body Rebuilds Itself From What You Give It

What you eat affects everything:

- Your physical energy
- Your mental clarity
- Your discipline and willpower
- Your sleep
- Your appearance
- Your hormones
- Your ability to perform under pressure

People think nutrition is just about getting "shredded" or dropping weight, but it's much bigger than that.

Your body literally rebuilds itself from the materials you give it. Your cells, your brain, your skin, your gut health-it's all being constructed from the choices you make with your fork.

Here are some core diet principles I keep in mind today:

1. **Protein First.** Start every meal with protein. It keeps you full, helps build muscle, and stabilizes your blood sugar.

   - Chicken, fish, eggs, steak, Greek yogurt, protein shakes
   - Aim for ~1g per pound of body weight daily, if you train regularly

2. **Whole Foods Win**

   - Prioritize real, minimally processed foods
   - Think vegetables, fruit, rice, oats, nuts, and healthy fats like olive oil or avocado
   - If it's processed, think twice about putting it into your body

3. **Limit Processed Foods and Sugar**

   - This doesn't mean "never," just don't let sugar and processed garbage become your default
   - A simple rule: If it comes in a box, bag, or drive-thru, eat it mindfully, not mindlessly

4. **Hydrate Like a Pro**

   - Start the day with a full glass of water before coffee
   - Drink at least half your body weight in ounces of water daily
   - Add electrolytes if you train hard or sweat a lot. I personally like Sugar free Liquid IV

5. **Meal Prep = Mental Peace**

   - Prepping meals for the week reduces stress, improves consistency, and prevents bad decisions

   - Sunday prep sessions make a difference- it's a ninety-minute investment that saves you money and sets your mindset up for the week.

Questions for Reflection

- What does my current diet say about how much I care about my goals?

- Do I treat food as fuel, or as a reward?

- What's one thing I can prep or replace this week that will simplify my nutrition?

- When have I felt my best? What was I eating (or not eating)?

STRIVE TO BE MEDICATION-LESS AT EIGHTY

Your health is a long game. The habits you build in your twenties and thirties either prevent pills, or guarantee them.

My Mom at Seventy

This lesson was inspired by watching my mom in her seventies. She still tries new things, moves around, and genuinely *wants* to live life to the fullest, not just survive.

She's the opposite of what most people expect from someone her age. While her friends are swapping stories about prescriptions, surgeries, or aches and pains, she's picking up new hobbies and constantly learning about AI. People think she's crazy when she says she wants to live to 120, and maybe she is. But she lives like someone who plans to make it, and that's something I admire. Her mindset, nutrition, and commitment to staying active keep her young. That's the kind of long-term energy I want to build for myself now, so I can *earn* that level of freedom later.

The Sad Reality

By retirement age, nearly 9 out of 10 adults take prescription medications in America. Heart disease, diabetes, high blood pressure, gut issues- these are all linked to poor lifestyle habits. Most of it is preventable before you get to the point of being your local pharmacy's best customer. You can either pay the price with discipline now, or pay the price with medication later.

Think Longterm

To avoid endless medications and side effects in your sixties and onward, you need a long-term strategy. Hoping for the best is not enough, you must **train for longevity, not ego**. What I mean by that is that you don't just want to chase a six-pack or endless marathon wins if it means you need a knee replacement by fifty-five. Listen to your body. Incorporate strength training and mobility to keep you functional.

Do the research or work with a trainer who wants to see you thriving when you're forty-five, not just in peak physical condition at twenty-five.

1. Build a Nutrition Strategy That's Sustainable

- You're not going to be tracking macros when you're 80 let's be honest so learn *how* to eat, not just *what* to eat

2. Prioritize Recovery and Stress Management

   - Sleep, hydration, sauna, movement, mindfulness-these are all medicine in their own way. Think of every night of solid sleep like taking a magical life extending pill

3. Use Supplements Wisely

   - You can't supplement your way out of bad habits but the right stack (like greens, creatine, magnesium, omega-3s) support longevity

4. Be Proactive With Health

   - Get your bloodwork done early and often. Make it normal to know what your blood pressure, blood type, and genetic predispositions are. Don't wait until something is *wrong* to finally decide to do something. Be proactive, not reactive

Imagine this: You're eighty. You wake up every morning after a good night of sleep with energy, loving life, excited to take on the day without any pills on your nightstand. You have no back pain, or doctor visits every other week. You're strong and ready to keep living as you were 40 years before then. You get there by starting early and staying consistent.

That future is built *right now.*

Questions for Reflection

- What kind of eighty-year-old do I want to be?
- What current habits would that version of me be proud of, or embarrassed by?
- What small daily change can I commit to making this week?
- How do I define "health" beyond just appearance?

MENTAL FITNESS IS JUST AS IMPORTANT AS PHYSICAL FITNESS

Your mental health is not separate from your physical health. They're interconnected systems that either strengthen or weaken each other. Just like you train your body, you need to actively train your mind for resilience, clarity, and emotional regulation.

For years, I treated my mental health as a secondary focus to physical fitness like they lived in separate boxes. It wasn't until I started paying attention to the patterns that I realized: my worst mental health days coincided with periods when I wasn't taking care of my body. And conversely, when my physical routine was dialed in, I handled stress better, slept deeper, and felt more emotionally stable.

The research backs this up: exercise releases endorphins, dopamine, and serotonin-your brain's natural antidepressants; but it goes deeper than that. When you prove to yourself that you can show up for a workout when you don't feel like it, you're building a mental toughness that carries into every other area of life.

A good book to dive into this more is *The Obstacle is the Way* by Ryan Holiday. It focuses on the practice of Stoicism in modern life. The goal being transforming adversity into advantage and achieving excellence through self-discipline. A lot of what Holiday writes about comes fromMarcus Aurelius, a Roman emperor who wrote *Meditations* as a private journal, not something he ever intended to publish. It was his personal reminder system, a place to come back to when things felt heavy or chaotic. He kept reinforcing the same idea over and over again: you don't control what happens to you, but you do control how you respond.

It's a mindset I've leaned on when things didn't go according to plan, and one that's helped me stay reflective instead of reactive.

Mental Fitness isn't Just "Thinking Positively"

Mental fitness isn't about toxic positivity or pretending everything is fine when it's not. It's about building practical skills to manage your internal thoughts and feelings.

I've learned that my mental health doesn't take care of itself. If I don't actively maintain it, it degrades, quietly at first, then all at once. That's why I built a simple daily routine around my mindset. Nothing extreme. Five to ten minutes in the morning to slow my brain down, before starting my work day. It's not about becoming some ultra-zen person. It's about creating a pause before the day starts pulling at me. At night, I do the opposite. I go to bed thinking about three things I'm genuinely grateful for. Some days it's a big win. Other days it's basic things like my health, my home, or just getting through a tough day. That small habit has been one of the fastest ways to quiet anxiety and keep me grounded.

Just as important has been learning how to manage my mental load. When my head feels cluttered, I don't try to power through it anymore. I do a brain dump. Everything on my mind goes on paper or in my notes app. Tasks, worries, random thoughts, all of it. The goal isn't to solve everything at that moment. It's to get it out of my head so it stops bouncing around. I've also had to get disciplined about boundaries with news and social media. Aside from the fact that it's distracting. Too much consumption on either leads to more stress, less focus, worse mood. Limiting what I consume has been one of the easiest ways to protect my mental energy without adding more work to my day.

And when I've needed extra support, I've stopped pretending I can handle everything alone. Therapy isn't a sign of weakness. That stigma would probably not be there as much if you called it having a mental coach in my opinion. No different than hiring a trainer if you want to get stronger physically. A therapist helps you understand your patterns, your blind spots, and the baggage you don't realize you're carrying. Worst case if you don't want to do therapy then talk to a friend that you think is a good person if something is on your mind and don't fight your battles internally. You should aim to treat mental health the same way as you treat everything else you care about.

Mental fitness and physical fitness aren't separate categories in my life. They feed each other. When I exercise consistently, everything upstairs works better. My stress levels drop because my body actually burns off the cortisol instead of letting it sit there all day. I sleep deeper, which makes the next day easier instead of feeling like I'm constantly catching up. My anxiety is lower, my mood is more stable, and I walk into conversations and challenges with more confidence. Even my thinking gets sharper. Decisions feel clearer. Problems feel smaller. Joe Rogan talks about this on his podcast. He knows that he tackles doing a cold plunge first thing in the morning; the rest of the day will be easier to manage because he already accomplished the hardest thing in his day and it was his choice to do so.

What surprised me most is how the relationship works in reverse too. When I'm taking care of my mental health, working out feels easier. I'm more motivated to show up instead of negotiating with myself. My recovery improves because I'm not constantly running on edge. I make better food choices without forcing it, sleep more consistently, and handle physical discomfort better because my mind isn't already exhausted. The workouts don't change, but my capacity to handle them does.

That's the real lesson. This isn't about choosing mental wellness or physical fitness. The most powerful approach is combining both. They create a positive feedback loop. A stronger body builds a calmer, more resilient mind. A calmer mind builds a stronger, more capable body. Ignore one and the other eventually suffers. Train both and everything in life feels more manageable.

Questions for Reflection

- How do I currently handle stress, and is it serving me well?
- When have I noticed the connection between my physical and mental state most clearly?
- What would change in my life if I treated mental fitness as seriously as physical fitness?
- Who in my life could I talk to about mental health without judgment?

CONSISTENCY IS A CHEAT CODE

Nothing beats consistency. Not motivation, not discipline on a good day, not a perfectly designed plan. If you want real results in fitness or in life, you have to show up again and again, especially when motivation fades, and that's the part most people don't want to talk about.

The hardest and most important lesson I've learned is that consistency isn't exciting. If you want a strong body, sustained energy, and real confidence, you have to get comfortable with small daily wins with no reward. There are no shortcuts and no thirty-day shreds that magically change your life. There's just showing up when you're tired, when you're busy, when your mind is telling you it's okay to skip, and when nobody is watching or cheering you on.

You might have heard or seen David Goggins video's on Youtube or read one of his books. He's a former Navy Seal who went from

300 lbs to a navy seal through pure determination and grit. He talks about days when he sits on the edge of his bed for thirty minutes, staring at his shoes before forcing himself to put them on and go for a run. Not because he feels motivated, but because he refuses to negotiate with himself. That's what consistency actually looks like. Telling your inner self to shut up and follow through with what it takes to achieve your goals. It isn't hype or emotion, it's action without debate.

This is where most people fall off. They work out for a week and wonder why their abs aren't showing. They eat clean for a few days and still feel bloated. They step on the scale, don't like the number, and decide it isn't worth it. What they fail to realize is that the results they want are months of consistency away, and every time they quit early, they reset the clock back to zero.

I learned this the hard way. There was a period when I stopped lifting for a while. Life got busy, travel picked up, and excuses crept in quietly, the way they always do. When I finally got back into the gym, my instinct was to go all in immediately, training harder and longer to make up for lost time. That mindset ends up getting you hurt if anything . I didn't need more intensity. I needed consistency, even when my schedule wasn't perfect.

What changed everything was when I heard a rule from Jocko Willink, another former Navy Seal badass: never miss more than two days in a row. One day is a miss. Two days becomes a pattern. That rule removed the pressure to be perfect and replaced it with something sustainable and easy to track. Over time, that rule creates consistency and accountability that adds up over time and compounds into results.

Making this stick is simple, but not easy. Schedule your workouts and treat them like meetings you don't cancel. Track your habits in a way that keeps you honest, whether that's a whiteboard, a notebook, or an app. Be ok with lowering the weight on the bar on hard days. If you don't feel like lifting, walk. If you don't feel like pushing hard, just show up and do something for 30 mins. Stack habits by linking workouts to things you already do, like waking up, grabbing coffee, or ending your workday. Most importantly, be okay with imperfect days, because consistent progress will always beat perfection.

Questions for Reflection

- What is one small thing I can commit to doing consistently each day for my health?
- Where in the past have I quit too early, and what excuse did I use at the time?
- What would change if I stopped chasing fast results and focused on steady progress instead?
- How can I track my consistency in a way that keeps me honest without burning me out?

FINANCE

COMPOUND GROWTH IS A MARVEL

Small, consistent financial habits lead to massive long-term gains. Compound growth isn't flashy, but it's the most powerful financial force you'll ever have access to if you let it work.

Chasing Fast Money vs. Building Real Wealth

I used to chase fast money. I wanted the big flip, the moonshot, the one move that would change everything overnight. Who doesn't? Especially in your twenties, I know I thought I was different and that if I could just get a good roll of the dice I'd make it.

That desire for fast money and easy wins kicks you in the teeth eventually. The classic Wall Street saying is "Bulls make money, bears make money, pigs get slaughtered" Extreme greed and chasing that extra little percentage gain bites you when the market turns and you don't know what you're doing.

During the GameStop mania, I made money so easily following the RoaringKitty mania throwing money into the market. I thought that's it? I just put money where this dude on the internet says he's investing and I can make 20, 30 60% gains? I remember waking up one morning with my trading account up fifty percent overnight. I genuinely thought I had cracked the code.

A few weeks later, that same account was worth less than what I started with. I wasn't building wealth, I was gambling and praying that I struck. That strike didn't come consistently and that's the problem. Everyone can have their lucky day in the markets, but to be consistent and beat the SP 500 on average is so hard to achieve. Unless you're a top trader at a big Wall Street Firm, it doesn't make sense to chase trades when you can consistently invest every paycheck and let compound growth do its thing.

Compound growth works better the less you interfere with it. It rewards patience, discipline, and time. It's the reason a janitor who saves consistently for forty years can retire a millionaire, while someone earning multi-six figures who never saves ends up stressed and living paycheck to paycheck.

If you invest just $500 a month into a low cost index fund starting at age twenty-five, earning a modest eight percent return, you end up with roughly $91,000 in ten years, about $295,000 in twenty years, and over $1.5 million in forty years. If you delay that start by ten years and you give up hundreds of thousands of dollars, simply because you waited.

That's the power of compounding. Time in the market beats timing the market.

The Order Matters More Than the Amount

Now before you start jumping into the investment world, one suggestion I highly recommend as you start to create your wealth plan is to follow a method for channeling your money. Knowing ahead of time where every dollar goes even as you increase income over time. I follow a simple income order of operations that keeps decisions clear and removes emotion from the process that I originally found on Youtube via the Tae Kim- Financial Tortoise channel.

First, you cover your basics. Build a small emergency fund so one unexpected expense doesn't send you into debt. Then, if your employer offers a 401(k) match, you contribute enough to get the full match, because that's free money and you never say no to free money.

Next comes high-interest debt. Credit cards, personal loans, anything with aggressive interest has to be paid off, because no investment reliably beats the guaranteed return of eliminating bad debt. That means paying off the statement balance every single month before you invest into other assets.

Once that's handled, you prioritize tax-advantaged accounts. Maxing out a Roth IRA comes next, because tax-free growth over decades is incredibly powerful. After that, you increase contributions to your 401(k) or similar retirement accounts until it's maxed out. If you're eligible, an HSA fits is a triple thread

Only after those bases are covered do you focus heavily on taxable investing, real estate, or more advanced strategies. The order matters because it protects you from trying to optimize before you've stabilized.

Types of Financial Accounts

- A Roth IRA is one of the best places to begin. You contribute after-tax money, but the growth and withdrawals in retirement are tax-free. When you're young, your biggest advantage is time, and a Roth lets compounding work without the IRS taking a cut later.

- Index funds are the backbone of long-term investing. Funds like VOO or VTI give you exposure to hundreds or thousands of companies at once, with low fees and no need to constantly trade. They're boring by design, and are easy to keep track of. Over time, the market rewards patience far more than prediction.

- Employer-sponsored plans like a 401(k) or 403(b) allow you to invest automatically, often with matching contributions. These accounts make consistency easier because the money is invested before you ever see it, which removes the temptation to spend it elsewhere.

- A Health Savings Account, if you qualify for one, is a quiet powerhouse. Contributions are tax-deductible, growth is tax-free, and withdrawals for qualified medical expenses aren't taxed either. Used correctly, it can function as both a healthcare buffer and an additional retirement account.
  - Pro tip- if you invest into an HSA and wait until 65 you can use any money saved in that account for any expenses not just healthcare related.
- High-yield savings accounts aren't about getting rich, they're about stability. They keep your emergency fund and short-term savings working for you instead of sitting idle, while still being accessible when life happens.

Once you master your ideal order of investing and stick to it, compound growth takes over. You stop trying to force results. You stop reacting to noise. You stop chasing the next shiny opportunity. Your job becomes simple, earn, allocate, repeat.

That's why compound growth is so powerful. It turns average decisions made consistently into extraordinary outcomes over time. It allows almost anyone, regardless of background, education, or starting point, to reach financial freedom if they stay the course long enough.

Your financial goals don't require genius. They require time and obedience to the process. Once the order is right, once the habits are locked in, wealth becomes less about effort and more about letting the system work.

Questions for Reflection

- Where in my financial life am I still chasing speed or excitement instead of letting a system run quietly in the background?

- Do I currently have an order for saving and investing, or am I making decisions reactively as money comes in?

- If I followed the same investing plan consistently for the next ten years, without changing it every time the market moved, where would that realistically put me?

  - Run the numbers

- How much less stress would I have if I stopped trying to pick the next stock, alt coin, or hot investment and let the market compound organically

THE DIFFERENCE BETWEEN GOOD DEBT VS. BAD DEBT

Debt gets a bad rap, but it's not inherently bad. It's a tool. Acquired blindly, it can wreck your life. Used strategically, it can build generational wealth. The key isn't to avoid debt, but to understand it.

The Expensive Education

When I first graduated college, I started making some money, and I did what everyone else did. I got a credit card... why not right? My mom and dad both had them. My friends all had one so I signed up for one under the guise of building my credit as so many of us do. It felt good, like I was making a clear step towards having good credit to eventually buy a home or start a business. The problem is that the ease of swiping the card with the bill coming later is a slippery slope.

Credit card companies make using cards so easy through technology, instant approvals and psychological hooks like rewards and delayed payments. This set up activates our brain's reward center, making spending feel less like debt and more about the pleasure in what you're buying. If you don't have self control you quickly become the credit card company's favorite customer paying 18-40% interest on purchases.

This has gotten even worse with buy now, pay later companies like Klarna and Affirm. Their business model isn't bad in essence but they take advantage of people's inability to have self control and lack of understanding of the difference between good and bad debt.

I remember the day I realized this was a sham. I was 27 years old, I was driving to my then girlfriend's house in the winter of 2019 making the minimum payment one month and realizing the interest alone was more than the entire payment. I called my brother and was like what is this? I paid my bill but my balance went up. That was the wake up call I needed to realize the trap I had fallen into. I got up the next day and made the decision to get out of debt no matter what it took.

Fast forward 3 months and Covid officially hit the USA. March 13th, 2020 my company at the time told us we'd be gone for two weeks at home waiting for this virus panic to die out and then we would be back at the office. We never went back and I moved back in with my mom. My goal was simple: Get out of debt, stack cash, and buy a home.

I cut every extra cost I could think of. I was buying sixty-count egg cartons at Walmart- six cents per egg- and eating eggs for breakfast, lunch, and dinner. That would last me a week. No bars, takeout, no treating myself. The only time this varied were the nights my mom felt bad for me and offered me some of whatever she had made that night. Every extra dollar went to crushing my credit card and student loan debt.

In one year and three months, I had done it:

- $7,600 in credit card debt: paid
- $36,000 in student loans: paid
- $16,000+ car loan: paid

I was officially debt free. It wasn't fun or glamorous.Honestly, it sucked. But I did what I set out to do and learned the difference between good and bad debt.

Good Debt

Now you might be asking yourself if credit cards are bad and buying a car with no material impact is bad debt ok, but what is good debt?

Good debt, often called strategic leverage, is debt that has the potential to increase your earning power, grow your net worth, or create long-term value when used intentionally. A mortgage on a home you live in or a rental property that cash flows can fall into this category, because the asset itself can grow in value over time while someone else, like a tenant, helps pay it down.

Student loans, when taken on wisely, can also be considered good debt when they lead directly to a high-return career. **A simple rule of thumb is that your first-year salary after completing your education should be greater than your total student loan balance.**

Business loans like a Small Business Administration loan (SBA) can be used to build income-producing assets or scalable streams of revenue can qualify as well, especially when the debt accelerates growth faster than saving alone would allow.

Even zero percent interest financing can be strategic when used with discipline, as long as the balance is paid off in full before interest kicks in and the cash you would have spent upfront is put to productive use elsewhere. The key distinction is that good debt works for you, not against you, and it only stays "good" when paired with clear intent, realistic returns, and the discipline to execute responsibly.

Questions for Reflection

- What debts are currently part of my life? Are they helping or hurting my goals?

- Have I ever experienced the snowball effect of bad debt? What did I learn from it?

- Could I be using good debt to build something—like buying a property or starting a business?

- What do I need to learn about debt, interest rates, or financing to make better decisions moving forward?

- Am I buying assets, or just buying time to impress people?

ZOOM OUT

One of the biggest mistakes young people make with money is zooming in too fast. You hear about a hot stock, crypto run, real estate play, or side hustle and feel like you need to act immediately or you'll miss your shot.

Before you invest in *anything*, you need to understand the environment you're investing in. That means zooming out.

The world moves in cycles. Interest rates go up and down. Inflation comes and goes. Certain industries grow while others slow. None of this is random. And if you ignore it, you end up fighting the current instead of riding it.

Why This Matters Early

When you're young, your biggest advantage isn't money, it's time. Compound growth only works if you stay in the game long enough. Constantly jumping from idea to idea, or investing because someone else made money, is how compounding gets interrupted before it ever has a chance to work.

Zooming out helps you avoid that.

It keeps you from forcing investments just because you feel behind. It helps you realize that sometimes the smartest move isn't buying something new, but building income, saving cash, and waiting for better conditions.

A Real Example

I had a plan to buy another house. I knew the strategy and was ready to move forward. By the time I was actually in position, interest rates had jumped, inventory dried up, and the numbers no longer made sense.

I didn't want to wait. But waiting was the right move.

So I rented, saved more, and reassessed. The goal didn't change, financial freedom through smart investing, but the method did. That decision protected my future instead of setting me back.

Different Ages, Same Rule

If you're early in your career, zooming out often means realizing that growing your income, building skills, and staying liquid matter more than picking the perfect investment right now.

If you're a little further along, it might mean resisting lifestyle upgrades so your money can compound instead of disappear.

No matter your age, the rule stays the same. Your goals stay fixed. Your methods stay flexible.

Compound growth only works when you let it run. Zooming out is how you avoid sabotaging it.

When you understand what's happening in the economy, you stop panicking during downturns and stop overreaching during hype cycles. You don't abandon your system every time the market shifts. You make calm adjustments instead of emotional ones.

That's how average people build wealth over time, not by being perfect, but by staying consistent and patient.

Some people make money in real estate. Others in stocks, business, or crypto. There's no single right path. What matters is choosing investments that make sense *right now*, based on where the world is going, not where it's already been.

Don't invest because your friend did. Don't invest because social media says you're late. Invest because the environment supports it, your financial order is solid, and you're thinking long-term.

Zooming out won't make you rich overnight. It will keep you from making mistakes that slow you down for years.

And in your twenties, that's everything.

Questions for Reflection

- Am I making financial decisions based on the big picture, or reacting to short-term noise?

- Where might patience protect my compound growth better than action right now?

- If the economic environment shifted tomorrow, would my system still hold up?

TIME IS MORE VALUABLE THAN MONEY

You can always earn more money, but you can't earn more time. Especially time with your loved ones.

The most valuable currency in the world is time. When you're young you have a LOT of it.

Personally, I'm still chasing success. I still work hard. I push every day towards the goal of being the best version of myself. I still want to hit big money goals. I want the car, the lakehouse, the boat, the endless trips. That part hasn't changed but I recognize that there are things that are worth more than chasing the next shiny object.

What *has* changed is my awareness of what I'm sacrificing in the process. When I was younger, I didn't think twice about pushing myself further and to squeeze in one more call. I thought that was what it took to be a winner. Winners never quit, and quitters never win. And to be fair, you often must have that mindset to achieve true success. I firmly think you must work your ass off upfront in order to enjoy your life later on. However, be careful in sacrificing what money can't buy in order to have time to make more money.

When you trade your *life* for your *lifestyle*, you have to ask if it's worth it.

The Truth About Wealth

They say young people want money, and wealthy people want time. That's not just a cute quote, it's the truth. Once your bills are paid, you've got your car, your house, your gym membership, your flights—then what?

Then you start realizing that time is the more valuable currency. Time with your family. Time with your friends. Time to breathe, to live, to reflect. The real flex isn't a luxury watch, it's having time to do what matters to you and what you want to do.

Think about it this way:

"Would you take $10 million today if it meant you die tomorrow?"

Of course not.

What about in a week? Probably not...

Okay, what about in a year or 10 years?

That question reveals the truth we all feel but rarely articulate: your time is more valuable than any amount of money. Yet we live like the opposite is true.

That's both the contradiction and the wake-up call.

This lesson isn't about quitting your job and running off to Bali to "find yourself." It's about moderation. IIt's about remembering that time is the *only* thing you never get back.

Once you're in your late twenties, thirties... people start spending less time with friends and extended family and start focusing on their own wants or family unit. The spontaneous hangouts disappear. The group trips slow down. And suddenly, you're in a stage of life where the *opportunity* for shared moments with friends shrinks.

Don't wait until it's too late to live life chasing another dollar. Go to the party. Make the trip. Go skydiving, Spend an extra hour with your mom before having to leave to take a meeting. with your dad. Watch your little cousin's soccer game. *Be in the present moment because as you get older you will wish you had.*

When you look back one day, it won't be your paychecks or promotions you think about. It'll be the memories you made with the people who matter most to you.

Questions for Reflection

- Am I sacrificing time for money in ways that don't align with my long-term values?

- If I had five more years to live, would I be happy with how I'm spending my days now?

CONTROL YOUR LIFESTYLE, OR IT WILL CONTROL YOU

One of the easiest ways to mess up your finances isn't bad investing or poor income, it's lifestyle creep. It sneaks in slowly, almost politely. You make more money, so your life gets a little nicer. Then a little nicer again. And before you realize it, every raise, bonus, or win gets absorbed into a higher cost of living.

It feels harmless at first. It even feels deserved. You worked hard, why shouldn't you enjoy it? And you should, to a point. The problem is when your lifestyle grows automatically instead of intentionally, especially when it's driven by comparison rather than actual need.

This is how people end up earning more than they ever thought possible and still feeling stuck.

Nobody really warns you about this part. They don't tell you that the pressure doesn't come from not having enough money, it comes from committing to a lifestyle that requires you to keep earning at a high level just to stay afloat. That's when money stops feeling like freedom and starts feeling like obligation.

I've watched it happen to a lot of people. New job, new apartment. Promotion, nicer car. Friends traveling more, so you travel more. None of it feels irresponsible on its own. But stacked together, it creates a life that's expensive to maintain and hard to step away from.

Keeping up with the Joneses is exhausting, and most of the Joneses are stressed too.

I've always tried to slow myself down when those upgrade urges hit. A big example of that was my car. I drove a Toyota Camry for over eight years. It was paid off, reliable, and completely unexciting. And honestly, that was the best part.

As my income increased, there were plenty of moments where I could have justified upgrading. Friends were driving nicer cars. I had hit milestones that felt like they deserved a reward. The temptation was always there. But every time I thought about buying something newer or flashier, I asked myself a simple question: does this actually improve my life, or does it just look like it does?

That Camry got me where I needed to go without adding stress, payments, or pressure. It let me save more, invest consistently, and build stability without feeling squeezed. When I finally bought my dream truck, it wasn't a stretch or an emotional decision. I could afford it comfortably, without changing my habits or sacrificing progress. That's the difference between buying something because you want it and buying it because you're ready.

Making more money doesn't mean you need to spend more money. In fact, the gap between what you earn and what you spend is where freedom begins. Every dollar you don't inflate your lifestyle with, gives you more flexibility.

This isn't about depriving yourself or pretending success doesn't matter. It's about being honest with yourself. Are you upgrading because it truly adds value to your life, or because it helps you feel like you've made it? Those two things aren't always the same.

People who control their lifestyle early don't always look impressive on the surface. They might drive older cars or live below what they can afford. But over time, they gain something far more valuable than appearances. They gain impulse control.

They can change jobs without panic. They can invest when others are scared. They can say no to things that don't align. They sleep better at night. They move through life with less urgency and more confidence.

On the other side, people who let their lifestyle grow unchecked often feel trapped by it. High income, high expenses, and no room to breathe. On paper, everything looks great. Behind the scenes, they are barely making it and the way society is in America it encourages this behavior.

Every purchase is a small decision that points you in one direction or another. Toward freedom or toward pressure. Toward calm or toward stress. You don't feel the impact right away, but you always feel it eventually.

The real flex isn't the car, the watch, or the house. It's having options in life. It's not needing to impress anyone. It's knowing that if something changes tomorrow, you'll be okay. That right there is what really matters. Freedom to do what you want to do and control over the options that are available.

If you've learned how compound growth works, understand the difference between good and bad debt, know when to zoom out, and respect your time, then controlling your lifestyle is what ties it all together.

KEEP COMING BACK

If you're reading this, you've made it to the end, and that alone says something. Thirty lessons before age thirty, not because life stops at thirty, but because this is usually when things begin to settle into place, when choices feel a little heavier and the direction you're moving in starts to matter more.

None of these lessons came from having everything figured out or following some perfect roadmap. They came from real experiences, from mistakes I didn't want to repeat, and from paying attention to what worked and what didn't, both in my own life and in the lives of people around me. Some of these lessons came easily, others took years to really understand, but all of them came from being willing to slow down and reflect.

If this book did anything, I hope it helped you think a bit more clearly about the kind of life you want to build and the choices that quietly shape it over time. Because life doesn't get simpler as you go, it gets louder. You get pulled in different directions. Old habits resurface. Expectations creep in. And sometimes you lose sight of what actually matters to you.

This book isn't meant to have all the answers. It's meant to be something you can return to when things feel off, when you need a moment to recalibrate, or when you just want a reminder of the principles you already know but sometimes forget to live by.

I come back to these lessons myself, not just when things are falling apart, but when I feel stuck, when I'm facing a decision without a clear right answer, or when I'm quietly questioning whether I'm still moving in the direction I want to be moving. Sometimes it's during a hard season, other times it's when life is going well and that's exactly when it's easiest to drift without realizing it. That's why I put these lessons together the way I did, not as rules to follow once and move on from, but as reminders to return to, recalibrate with, and use as a checkpoint along the way. My hope is that you treat this book the same way, something you come back to when you need perspective, when you need grounding, or when you just want to make sure you're still choosing your life intentionally.

Whether you're twenty-three or thirty-nine, these lessons don't stop applying, they just take on new meaning as your life changes. You'll read them differently at different stages, and that's exactly how it should be. This book is meant to grow with you, not sit on a shelf.

If your twenties were about exploring and learning, your thirties tend to be about living more intentionally, making choices that reflect who you are rather than who you think you're supposed to be. It becomes less about chasing and more about aligning, less about proving and more about protecting what matters.

So keep setting goals that feel honest. Take care of your body and financial well being. Be mindful of what you give your time to and who you give it to. And when life throws something unexpected your way, as it inevitably will, don't rush to fix everything at once. Just slow down and come back to what grounds you.

Flip through a few pages. Revisit a lesson that stood out. Sit with the questions without needing immediate answers. Remind yourself that growth isn't linear and that drifting doesn't mean you're lost.

You don't need to have everything figured out. Most people never do. You just need to keep paying attention, making small adjustments, and coming back to yourself when you wander.

That's how this book came together.

And that's how a good life is built.

ABOUT THE AUTHOR

I didn't follow a traditional Millennial American path, and that's exactly why I see things the way I do.

I was born in Switzerland, spent my early childhood in Como, Italy, and moved to the United States when I was six. Growing up with one foot in Italian culture and the other in American culture taught me something early on, there are multiple ways to live a good life. What works in one place doesn't always translate to another. That dual perspective made me question convention, not out of rebellion, but out of curiosity, I wanted to figure out what actually worked for me instead of blindly following a cultural script.

School was never my thing. I couldn't sit still, I had too much energy, too many questions about life, and not enough patience for a desk and a chalkboard. By the time I graduated high school, the only place that really made sense to me was the gym. It was simple. Input equaled output. Show up, put in the work, see results. I liked the truth in that process that you couldn't hide from. Something that didn't translate into other parts of life, which for me at 18 years old applied to my high school journey and what was next.

Six months after missing the fall college application window, my mom sat me down for a long conversation, one of those quiet moments that ends up changing everything. She asked me to give college a shot first, to get an education, and then, if I still wanted to join the military, I could. I'm grateful every day that I listened.

What followed was a decade in SaaS sales that taught me more about life than any classroom ever could. I went from making a hundred cold calls a day, hoping someone wouldn't hang up in the first ten seconds, to leading enterprise conversations as a trusted advisor inside a growing startup. Along the way, sales forced me to understand people, build trust, read situations, adapt quickly, and take rejection without losing momentum. That career was built through real conversations, real failures, and real wins, and somewhere in that process I realized something important.

There's a massive gap between what we're taught and what we actually need to know.

No one teaches you how to navigate relationships, build wealth, stay healthy, or make decisions that align with your values. You're expected to just figure it out. That's what I did, sometimes through my own mistakes, sometimes by watching others win big or crash hard, always by asking questions and paying attention.

30 Under 30 came from that process.

It started as notes in my phone, reminders to myself about lessons I didn't want to forget. Over time, it turned into something bigger, a way to help others avoid learning everything the hard way. This is the book I wish someone had handed me at eighteen, or even at twenty-eight. It's not theory from someone who figured life out decades ago and forgot what struggle feels like. It's real-time perspective from someone still in the arena, still learning, but far enough along to recognize the patterns that actually matter